Praise for
The God Who Hates I
Confronting & Rethinking Jew

"David Hartman inhabits the places of the impossible—where truths collide—with courage. A traditional and halakhic Judaism will emerge from its clash with the ethical more faithful to its essence."
—**Rabbi Shira Milgrom**, Congregation Kol Ami, White Plains, New York

"A masterful, passionate confessional of an encounter in one man's soul between traditional Judaism and his deepest moral sensibilities. Whether or not you agree with Rabbi Hartman's vision, this book will pursue you long after you have read it."
—**Yehuda (Jerome) Gellman**, Ben-Gurion University of the Negev

"Another essential and prophetic work from one of the great religious thinkers of the age. This deeply felt book is intensely personal yet intellectually rigorous—a challenge and a consolation for everyone who looks for God."
—**James Carroll**, author, *Jerusalem, Jerusalem: How the Ancient City Ignited Our Modern World*

"This is the book from David Hartman we have been waiting for! Written with passion, clarity, and scholarship … [it] is sure to provoke a lively conversation on the nature of Jewish law, the State of Israel and what it means to live in a covenanted relationship with God."
—**Rabbi Elliot J. Cosgrove, PhD**, Park Avenue Synagogue; editor, *Jewish Theology in Our Time: A New Generation Explores the Foundations and Future of Jewish Belief*

"A trenchant and controversial statement of Jewish theology.… No thinking Jew can afford to ignore this book."
—**Rabbi Neil Gillman, PhD**, emeritus professor of Jewish philosophy, The Jewish Theological Seminary of America; author, *Doing Jewish Theology: God, Torah and Israel in Modern Judaism*

The GOD WHO HATES LIES

Jewish Lights Books by Dr. David Hartman

From Defender to Critic:
The Search for a New Jewish Self

The God Who Hates Lies:
Confronting and Rethinking Jewish Tradition

A Heart of Many Rooms:
Celebrating the Many Voices within Judaism

A Living Covenant:
The Innovative Spirit in Traditional Judaism

Love and Terror in the God Encounter:
The Theological Legacy of Rabbi Joseph B. Soloveitchik

The GOD WHO HATES LIES

Confronting & Rethinking Jewish Tradition

DAVID HARTMAN

WITH
CHARLIE BUCKHOLTZ

For People of All Faiths, All Backgrounds

JEWISH LIGHTS Publishing

Woodstock, Vermont

The God Who Hates Lies:
Confronting and Rethinking Jewish Tradition

2014 Quality Paperback Edition, First Printing

Scripture quotations are from *Tanakh* (Philadelphia: Jewish Publication Society, 1985), unless otherwise noted.

© 2011 by David Hartman

Library of Congress Cataloging-in-Publication Data
Hartman, David, 1931–
The god who hates lies : confronting and rethinking Jewish tradition / David Hartman with Charlie Buckholtz.
p. cm.
Includes bibliographical references.
ISBN 978-1-58023-455-9 (hardcover)
1. Jewish law—Philosophy. 2. Jewish ethics—Philosophy. 3. Orthodox Judaism—Philosophy. 4. Judaism—Doctrines. I. Buckholtz, Charlie. II. Title.
BM520.6.H37 2011
296.3'6—dc22
2011004740

ISBN 978-158023-790-1 (paperback)
ISBN 978-158023-598-3 (eBook)

10 9 8 7 6 5 4 3 2 1
Manufactured in the United States of America
Cover design: Tim Holtz

Published by Jewish Lights Publishing
A Division of Longhill Partners, Inc.
Sunset Farm Offices, Route 4, P.O. Box 237
Woodstock, VT 05091
Tel: (802) 457-4000   Fax: (802) 457-4004
www.jewishlights.com

CONTENTS

Introduction

"What Planet Are You From?"

A Yeshiva Boy's Pilgrimage into Philosophy, History, and Reality

Before moving to Israel with my family in 1971, in the afterglow of the Six-Day War, I served for sixteen years as a congregational rabbi. During that time, I did all the things traditional rabbis do: taught classes, led services, officiated life-cycle events, gave sermons, and counseled people seeking guidance in the religious dimension of their personal lives. In these conversations I heard people sincerely struggling with all manner of inner conflict. One recurring theme was the agonizing confrontation that occurred when religious demands were felt to conflict with deeply held relational commitments and ethical intuitions. I was so moved by so many of these stories that I began to sense they reflected not only the natural limitations of any legal system, but deep fissures in the edifice of Jewish tradition, both the culture within which it had been formed and the culture that saw itself as the steward of tradition's authentic legacy. I attempted to address my congregants' concerns with as much religious creativity and empathic humanity as I could muster. Meanwhile I was collecting my own set of questions and conflicts.

That this type of personal religious conflict did not grow into a major theme of my rabbinate was on no account due, then, to anything like a lack of interest or concern. I chalk it up rather to the intervention of global-historical forces. In the time leading up to my *aliyah*, my attention had become increasingly focused on the possibilities for national Jewish renaissance presented by the still new reality of the Jewish state, with what I vividly imagined as its wide-open field of new spiritual and moral possibilities. My sermons in North America focused largely, and energetically, on weaving pictures of how this renaissance might take shape. I thought of the Jewish state as a redemptive opportunity for the political implementation of Jewish social aspirations in the context of a sovereign public. I spoke excitedly about the religious significance of a society not only shaped by the Jewish people, or even a Jewish ethos in a general sense, but organized politically around the creative contemporary application of biblical and Rabbinic categories of social justice.

In Israel, I deeply believed, we would have a socioeconomic system that implements the spirit of the biblical and Rabbinic laws of *shmita*, the seven-year cycle of debt forgiveness intended to mitigate the loss of dignity that comes with excessive dependency on creditors. I had heard that financial pressures in Israel made it necessary for many parents to take out loans to support their newly married children and provide for the necessities required to start a new family. In many of my sermons, I suggested that it would be in the spirit of the Torah—if perhaps not in the precise legal framework of *shmita*—for the Israeli government to implement a policy that would mandate Israeli banks to lower interest rates every seven years. Similarly the biblical jubilee, a fifty-year cycle culminating in a celebratory emancipation of slaves and redistribution of property (families who, because of poverty, have been forced to sell their land within this cycle, are reinstated to their former homesteads) that strives to set the conditions for a society free of economic disparity. This egalitarian spirit could be translated into social policies intent on offering possibilities for personal economic renewal, safeguarding hope for the future in those who might otherwise have good reason to despair.

I often proclaimed, and sincerely believed, that Israel would be a place where we could witness the ethical spirit of Torah manifested in a sovereign Jewish society.

In retrospect, the rude awakening I encountered upon my arrival was perhaps inevitable. It was brought home to me with characteristic Israeli bluntness in a conversation with a cabdriver a year or two into my move. The *shmita* year was approaching, and I saw that the concern among many Orthodox Jews in the country had little to do with restoring financial dignity to those in need. The focus, instead, was on kashrut, the permissibility or impermissibility of certain foods. Another facet of *shmita* law (the term literally means "release") entails that every seven years Jewish-owned fields in Israel must be left to lie fallow, their produce considered ownerless and prohibited from being bought or sold. Given this restriction, Israeli farmers were not permitted to cultivate their fields, leaving Israeli citizens to buy only from farmers outside of Israel, primarily Arab farmers in the West Bank and Jordan. The predominant, passionate, and at times vicious discourse within much of the religious community concerned whether various halakhic loopholes, whose purpose was to allow Israelis to buy Israeli-farmed produce, easing the strain of the *shmita* law upon the fledgling Jewish economy, could be considered legitimate and trustworthy. The halakhic tradition has an esteemed history of generating such creative legal fictions in times of communal need, and the contemporary rabbis responsible for and supportive of those pertaining to *shmita* were among the most respected in the country, otherwise widely revered. Nevertheless, battle lines were drawn astride the issue of whether food cultivated and sold based on these legal solutions could be considered kosher.

Meanwhile, riding in my taxi through the streets of Jerusalem, we passed restaurants featuring signs proudly proclaiming, "We observe *shmita le-chumra*"—that is, in its strictest form (the implicit message being: without relying on any loopholes tainted with a nationalist spirit). Jews only seemed to be able to handle the expansive spirit of tradition by confining it to questions of what foods may or may not be eaten, whose establishments could be patronized, which homes adhered to sufficiently strict dietary codes as to permit sharing their bread (or fruit). Where I had hoped and expected to find a national moral renaissance, I found instead a Rabbinate stuffing halakhic practice with dubious stringencies based on a rejectionist reflex I could not fathom, crowding out and when necessary shouting down the possibility of alternate religious voices, conversations, and priorities.

I spent the majority of my taxi ride haranguing the driver with my disgust for the small-minded way in which Torah principles were being assimilated into the national religious consciousness, and regaling him with my vision for how it might be otherwise. When I had finished— or perhaps merely paused for a breath—he turned to me and said he only had one question. Of course, I was eager to hear it. He spoke in Hebrew:

"What planet are you from?"

I knew what he meant. I also felt I was on a very different planet, not only from the one I had envisioned as a congregational rabbi in North America, but from the one I shared with my fellow Israelis. The ultra-Orthodox *haredim* were adamant in their refusal to acknowledge that the founding of the modern state held any fundamental significance for adherents of the ancient tradition or demanded any new or creative responses from the rabbis responsible for shaping Jewish law. To the contrary, their single-minded commitment seemed to be re-creating a shtetl in the form of a state.

As a religious person and a Zionist, I thought I might have better luck with the Religious Zionist community in Israel. But I felt no greater affinity with their attribution of messianic meaning to Israel's rebirth than I had with the militant-*haredi* refusal to attribute any spiritual meaning to it at all. I could no more buy into the religious-nationalists' providential theology of historical and political processes than I could the patronizing significance they assigned to the secular Zionist revolution: their claim, for example, that just as God used non-Jews to build the ancient Temple, so too now He was using the waves of secular *olim* as foot soldiers in the march toward messianic redemption. Viewing secular Jews as unwitting instruments of religious triumphalism seemed to me neither inspiring nor inclusive, notwithstanding the good intentions of many touting this vile apologetics.

Neither could I muster much enthusiasm for the delusional triumphalism of Israeli secularists, their belief that living in Israel was the solution for the assimilationist trend in North America. Among this group, the hostility toward traditionalism of any form was palpable, and their collective political life was devoid of religious thinking or meaning.

Not long into my *aliyah*, a renowned and beloved leader of the kibbutz movement invited me to speak to the youth of his own kibbutz. During my lecture, I noticed that they seemed to be exclusively focused not on my words, but on the round piece of fabric on top of my head. The kibbutz leader was compelled to exhort them, "Don't judge him by his *kippah!*" while attempting to reassure them that I was not a member of the Religious Zionist establishment they had been trained to revile. This was the first time in my life that I had ever experienced my *kippah* as a barrier to being listened to—something that had never happened in North America over the many opportunities I had to speak with non-traditional Jews. I was forced to ask myself, *if I want to reach out to secular Israelis, to meet and study with them, do I have to remove my* kippah? The idea seemed perverse. I had studied for five years with the Jesuits in Fordham University and felt perfectly comfortable and accepted wearing my *kippah* in all my classes there. Could it be that now, in order to be taken seriously in the Jewish homeland, I would have to remove it?

And yet, in a conversation with Ezer Weizman, the president glowed, and gloated, that Israel had "solved" the problem of assimilation and Jewish identity. This was a familiar line espoused by Israeli leaders who seemed to consider it a strong argument for *aliyah*. Personally, I found it amazing that anyone actually living in this country could make such a claim while maintaining a straight face. I responded to Weizman that one learns a lot about the quality of a person's home—and the values of their family—by their behavior when they leave. "Look how Israelis live in North America," I said, noting a phenomenon I had observed consistently over my time as a rabbi there: the tendency of Israelis to live largely as alienated outsiders to the Jewish community, finding it extremely difficult to identify with

Jewish communal life beyond the cultural paradigms of the state itself. Aside from eating falafel and reading Hebrew-language newspapers, there seemed to be little that connected them to the larger Jewish community outside of Israel.

As a religious Jew, what did Israel mean to me? I felt at times that I had fallen victim to my own lofty Zionist-religious fantasies and in darker moods wished I had followed the lead of many of my congregants and tuned out the impassioned sermons I had given in my erstwhile home. Why had I come?

Most of my thinking and writing in the intervening years—now decades—has been a response to the internal conundrums brought on by this challenging state of affairs. How, as a religious Jew, could I explain my attachment to the political forces that created the State of Israel, a movement of rebellion against traditional Judaism, without recourse to self-aggrandizing, messianic mythologies that I found intellectually and morally bankrupt? The Religious Zionists' grandiose claims of representing the exclusive authentic continuity of Jewish history rang false in my ears. However, the reality of Israel itself had already exposed the many weaknesses of the Eastern European, yeshiva-based traditionalism upon which I had been educated and raised. How, as a Zionist, could I explain my attachment to religious traditionalism, whose conservative tendencies threatened to smother the cultural rebirth Jewish political sovereignty made possible—and which, in my view, was desperately needed both for the State of Israel and for the state of Judaism worldwide?

In response, I developed a theology, based on the concept of covenant, that understands the relationship between God and the Jewish people as one of intimacy and partnership. This covenantal model—in which God not only tolerates but demands and delights in Jews' taking of responsibility for ever-increasing dimensions of our individual and collective lives, infusing every element of human endeavor and experience with religious meaning and purpose—describes a religious anthropology characterized not by slavishness and a howling sense of inadequacy in the face of an infinite commanding God. Instead it resurrects the vital and precocious religious spirit of the

Talmudic Rabbis, who understood that the implementation of God's will amid the complex considerations of human society and psyche requires, at times, the full and fearless assertion of our intellectual independence. The covenant struck between God and the Jewish people was not exclusively a call to unconditional obedience; it was equally a call to empowerment and an affirmation of human adequacy. Within this covenantal theology, the Zionist enterprise could be understood not as a rebellion against the tradition, but as an exciting new stage of covenantal responsibility. The Jewish people, energized by the halakhic system's inventive capacity to apply the aspirational ethics of biblical mitzvah to any socio-historical reality in which Jews find themselves, would expand that category to include social and political functions of which two thousand years of exiled wandering had stripped them. These new varieties of responsibility would require new responses from the halakhic system, but this dynamic religious evolution would constitute the realization of covenantal consciousness *sine qua non*. The new stage of covenant would bring forms of personal and collective religious dignity yet unknown in Jewish history. Not only was the Torah no longer in heaven, as the Talmudic Rabbis declared, having been given over to human hands at Sinai; so too, the covenantal understanding of Israel's rebirth taught us that the direction of history was now included within the scope of human responsibility. Instead of passively waiting for the coming of the Messiah to initiate the ingathering of the exiles, secular Zionists had sparked a new understanding of the covenantal rebirth of Israel.

Intuition versus Tradition

It would be difficult to understate the extent to which my hope for a renaissance of halakhic innovation, nurtured and energized by Jewish sovereignty, has remained, as yet, unrealized. To the contrary, it does not take a particularly keen observer of the Israeli religious scene to note a steady and at times seemingly inexorable regression to Eastern European attitudes and norms. Driven with a ruthlessly utopian sense of purpose by the *haredi* community, it is a movement whose influence continues to expand with their ever-increasing numbers and political clout. Meanwhile, all the national-religious myths of a messianic renaissance—so imminent, so immanent, if only we were truly willing to sacrifice ourselves (and our children) for the Land—hold as little interest for me as ever.

In the intervening years, I established a research and teaching institute, as well as a high school, devoted to the kind of creative, questioning, open-ended religious thinking from which I feel the state, and the Jewish people, might greatly benefit. I have elaborated my own thinking over the course of several books and scores of lectures, and the Shalom Hartman Institute continues to encourage research, support scholars, publish work, and teach students in this spirit. Not unlike the Jews themselves, it is a community whose voice in the public arena is disproportionately strong for its size. It is a place people know they can come to study and discuss their tradition, where no question is out of bounds and no part of the self must be checked at the door as the price of admission into the Jewish conversation.

In the meantime, after decades dominated by an engagement with the sweeping themes and collective drama of Jewish history, my own thoughts have turned back to the more intimate religious questions characteristic of those I used to encounter in my counseling capacity as a congregational rabbi and have continued to encounter as a teacher and lecturer in Jerusalem and abroad. Many of these proved so compelling that I was moved to take them on as my own; others set off domino chains of analogous questions, no less vexing, particular to my own experience and temperament. My political thinking is a matter of public record; to whatever extent it may influence or elude public discourse, I still live daily as an individual. I am still confronted with conflicts and required to make choices. Where am I going to pray, and with whom? How am I going to relate to the parts of my extended family that have a different interpretation of Judaism than I do, informed by values that in some cases I find abhorrent?

To state the question in a broader, more essential form: How do I justify maintaining a commitment to the Jewish religious tradition in the places where it demands I violate what I intuitively feel and know? What place, if any, does my personal, subjective intuition have in a halakhic system—not just abstractly, but for someone who wants to live, day to day, within that system?

I have long felt that the covenantal framework, fundamentally a theology of empowerment, has great potential for application beyond the political sphere. This book is an attempt to flesh out some aspects of what covenantal theology might look like applied to questions of inner religious conflict. My loyalty to the tradition, after all, is not limited to its implications for the modern State of Israel. What does it mean for my religious struggles, for the conflicts I encounter between morality and halakha? What does it mean for an individual who finds that certain cherished moral values are being uprooted by the same tradition that in other areas manages to inspire great love, loyalty, and faith? What does it mean for the individual who stands committed to that tradition, yet at the same time knows what he or she knows, and cannot manage to be other than who he or she is?

The kinds of questions to which I am referring span a wide range of human experience and religious concern. I would like to present a few examples, some of which I will explore in greater detail in the following chapters.

As a congregational rabbi I once faced an issue involving a psychiatrist who was also a *kohen* (pl. *kohanim*), meaning his family tradition held that he was a descendent of the priestly class. According to halakha, *kohanim* face more restrictive marriage laws than other Jews and are prohibited, for example, from marrying women who have converted to Judaism. This particular *kohen* had been searching for a life partner for twenty years and had finally found a woman—*the* woman—he wanted to share his life with. He came to me one day, full of joy at this news: he would finally be able to build a family. Thus, I was surprised when he came to speak to me again the following week and his face was despondent; he seemed like someone lost in a dark, empty room, nearly devoid of hope. I sensed his anxiety and pain, acutely and viscerally, before he opened his mouth. Then he explained: this woman was a convert to Judaism. He had been told by religious friends whom he trusted that the tradition's position on this matter was unequivocally clear: by virtue of her former life as a non-Jew, this woman would forever be taxonomized by Jewish law as a *zona*, a woman reasonably suspected of sexual promiscuity and therefore unfit for marriage to a priest. I felt the tragedy of the situation, his personal devastation. It seemed dishonest not at least to ask the question: Is this traditional status indeed irrevocable? Could this really be God's will? (See chapter 4.)

Similarly, the Torah places *mamzerim*, children born out of sexual relations it categorizes as illicit, into a highly restrictive marriage category: they can only marry each other, and non-*mamzerim* are prohibited from marrying them. In sermons and classes, I would decry the lamentable ethical implications of giving divine imprimatur to such stigmatization. In response, I was often asked how far I was willing to carry this critique. Would I marry my child to a *mamzer*? By the same token, having become known for my passionate espousal of religious pluralism, to this day I am often asked (not infrequently in a challenging tone): Would I personally accept conversion from a Conservative or Reform rabbi? Would I endorse the marriage of my daughter to someone with such a conversion? If not, where is my commitment to pluralism; does it have any behavioral implications? I have been criticized that it is not sufficient to speak of tolerance in the abstract; what is it, I am asked, that I am prepared to *do*? Are there areas in which my philosophical commitment to pluralism trumps my covenantal commitment to current formulations of halakha? (See chapter 2.)

Another area in which tradition often comes into conflict with ethical intuition concerns the role and treatment of women within traditional Jewish frameworks. To take one example that is literally close to home, several years ago my daughter Tova helped to found an egalitarian Orthodox synagogue in Jerusalem dedicated to infusing the prayer community with a feminist ethos. I am often asked by more "mainstream" modern Orthodox Jews, "as a student of Rav Soloveitchik" (who would likely have opposed such an innovation), how can I justify davening in my daughter's synagogue, where women chant the service, read from the Torah, and give sermons? Well ... how can I? Sometimes I answer anecdotally, though this approach presents clear limits. When asked by an ultra-Orthodox nephew how I justify my presence at my daughter's shul, I told him, "I feel the *shekhina* [i.e., the feminine emanation of God's presence] singing with the women's voices." My nephew responded in kind, answering that if there is one thing he is certain of, it is that the *shekhina* is not in that place. How can such a service have religious meaning if it violates the traditional role of women in Judaism? (See chapter 3.)

Another challenging area concerns the extent to which we allow changing historical realities to alter deeply embedded ritual categories. To state the question bluntly: how much weight do we give reality in defining Jewish practice? An Israeli high school student approached me, bothered by the question of why we continue to celebrate the holiday of Tisha B'Av—the Jewish calendar's most profound day of mourning, commemorating of the destruction of the ancient Temple, the loss of Jewish sovereignty in Israel, and the exile from Jerusalem. "What's the problem?" I asked. "Well," the student replied, "look at the prayers!"

> Comfort, Lord our God, the mourners of Zion, and the mourners of Jerusalem, and the city that is mournful and ruined, humiliated and desolate: mournful without her children, ruined without her dwellings, humiliated without her dignity, and desolate without a single occupant …

"They speak, in the present tense, of the destruction and desolation of Jerusalem while we, who live in Jerusalem, can look out our windows and see clearly that this is not the case." How, he wanted to know, can we continue to speak these falsehoods? Can we leave it out, if speaking such words offends our sense of reality and thus the integrity of our prayer? Can reality trump the legal formalism that at times renders certain ritual practices not only ethically, but emotionally and/or intellectually incoherent? (See chapter 5.)

A separate but related, and critically important, question: what weight do we give solidarity to define membership in the Jewish community? Newly arrived immigrants from the former Soviet Union, inducted as soldiers in the Israeli army, quickly encounter the religious culture of an institutional Rabbinate dominated by *haredi* insularity and rejection-ism. The soldiers often ask me, "Professor Hartman, do you accept me as a Jew in good standing, or do I have to bring some sort of proof that my maternal great-grandmother was a Jew? Isn't serving in the army sufficient grounds for accepting me as a member of the Jewish family?"

The grotesque cruelty to which this kind of insular and highly formalistic religious thinking so often leads was recently brought home to me in a conversation with a soldier who had immigrated to Israel from Ukraine. The soldier did not attempt to hide his anger toward the State of Israel: "I was more religiously observant in the Ukraine than here!" he would exclaim, clearly bewildered and embittered by this strange paradox. Yet he refused to step foot into a synagogue in Israel. I asked him to explain why. It turned out that he had seen a close friend, also a Russian immigrant, killed in battle while serving along-side him in the army. Shortly after his friend's heroic death, the religious authorities in charge of burial began asking questions about his lineage—perhaps his grandmother could be confirmed Jewish, but what about his great-grandmother?—that called into question whether he would be entitled to burial in a Jewish cemetery. "They saw him as enough of a Jew to die for the country," the soldier ruefully remarked, "but not enough of a Jew to be buried in it." How can we respond in the places where dominant religious culture seems so at odds with its own basic values that it creates grotesque violations of decency and trust? (See chapter 6.)

In a similar vein, I find myself considering the persistent tensions I encounter within myself, between my own sense of solidarity with Jews who serve in the army and my feelings of alienation toward obser-vant Jews who remain staunchly indifferent to the religious signifi-cance of such a total commitment of self. This struggle has pointed resonances within my own biography. Growing up, my older brother was my *rebbe*: a father figure, religious teacher, and confidant. Much of my own deep feeling for and commitment to Jewish tradition and the Torah world—and certainly my acute sense of love and responsibility for the Jewish people—is a result of his influence and example. My brother identified with the *haredi* community in Israel, known, among other social markers, for refusing to send their children to the army. My children did serve in the army, and over time—seeing what my children were exposed to, while yeshiva students walked around smugly immune to such dangers—it became difficult to look at my brother in the same way I once had, to maintain the same intimacy, compassion, and friendship we had once shared. When my daughter was under the *huppah* with her future husband, a pilot in the Israeli Air Force, I could not bring myself to invite my older brother to stand under the wedding canopy with the rest of the family. As a result of that experience, I realized how deeply estranged I was from the yeshiva world that had nurtured me and given so much meaning to my life. I felt greater solidarity with so-called secular Israelis prepared to give up their lives for the security and well-being of Israeli society, than with the yeshiva world who maintain that Torah study alone is sufficient to protect the Jewish people in Israel. I knew there were serious philosophical and religious implications to this deep estrangement. But I could not articulate them and did not yet know what form they should take.

As I mentioned above, in the past these kinds of questions had provoked mainly gut feelings and responses of a speculative, intuitive nature. I have come to feel that a more systematic approach is both necessary and possible. As a traditional Jew unwilling to surrender my critical faculties when entering the religious conversation, confronted with ideas and practices I cannot simply buy "on faith," I do not feel that I am alone. Decades of experience as a rabbi and teacher, hundreds of conversations with people facing similar types of conflicts from across the religious spectrum, have shown me that I am not.

The Path of My Theology

What is the weight of tradition when it conflicts with one's deep moral sense? How does one maintain membership in the halakhic community while acting against the authoritative tradition? Is making choices that favor moral convictions equivalent to stepping out of the tradition? Conversely, to yield to the tradition, squelch the ethical impulse … what is lost? What is lost personally, what is lost to the community, and what is lost to the religion itself?

In the following pages, I will attempt to provide an intellectual framework for addressing these theological questions and applying them to one's religious life. In doing so, I draw upon a lifetime of learning, teaching, and experience both within Jewish tradition and without. My intensive Orthodox yeshiva background, while deeply enriching, did not train me to analyze the tradition with any sort of critical tools. Indeed, any form of distance between tradition and self was seen by that community as a spiritual fault. And so in some ways, this book tracks my own intellectual and spiritual development, the spiritual search of a committed yeshiva boy and party-line Orthodox rabbi who discovered, and has been deeply impacted by, tools and insights drawn from other spiritual and intellectual traditions.

In the yeshiva world of my upbringing, religious issues were both consuming and studiously circumscribed to the personal sphere. Can I daven with more *kavana* (spiritual focus) than I have thus far managed to muster? Can I, in the model of legendary rabbis like the Vilna Gaon, commit uncompromisingly to limiting *bitul Torah* (interruption of Torah study); am I devoting all my time, energy, and intellectual potential to the only pursuit of any value, *talmud Torah* (Torah study)? Beyond the devotion to study, the struggles dominating this rigorous spiritual path center around how compelling one experiences the pull to perform mitzvot in all their expansive and exacting detail. This is a deeply personal religiosity, shaped by the communal standards of traditional halakha, which is adequate and sufficient unto itself. The tradition can only be undermined by a given individual's lack of clarity, focus, and will.

And so it was that as a yeshiva *bachur* (single Jewish male), my passion was single-minded: to study Torah, and in particular to engage the Talmud, absorbing the analytical insights of the great religious leaders of the past. Those rabbis whose teachings and insights were assimilated into the yeshiva world were the only significant interlocutors I encountered. I loved them, and I loved the world in which I met them: its intensity; its warmth; its sense of righteous camaraderie; its self-understanding as the sole legitimate address of all that is important, life's essential truth and meaning. I felt while in yeshiva that I was always on the right path, a true, authentic historical path that nurtured the Jewish people and gave meaning to their everyday life. I never confronted, with any depth, the idea of God or how one comes to accept a life devoted to the service of God. I found the Jewish God when I found the Jewish people, studying in the *beit midrash*, where I experienced the reality of a robust and bracing religious life within the context of others committed to the same path. It was the living community of yeshiva students that mediated the possibilities for religious introspection and growth.

My own religious growth was measured exclusively by dedication to mastering the intellectual tradition of the Talmud: to formulate new *svaras* (analytical frames used to resolve Talmudic self-contradictions and unify disputes) and *hiddushim* (novel insights). Offering a conceptual breakthrough to explain a seemingly intractable disagreement between Maimonides and Ravad—this was literally my raison d'etre. At the time it did not occur to me that the innovative mind of the yeshiva *bachur*, always active and engaged, is enlisted *exclusively* to clarify the internal contradictions and disagreements within the system. For example, we never asked second-order questions: What is the epistemological basis of a given disagreement? What part of the tradition should be ascribed to revelation, what part to human creativity, and what might be the implications of how this question is answered for the development of communal religious practice? Instead I found that the received tradition in its entirety was ascribed to revelation— that all norms, including the customs and cultural quirks of recent generations, had become divinely sanctioned as somehow included within the mysterious revelatory moment of Sinai. The question of what that moment contained, and what it left for future generations of human creativity to discover, is preempted by the assertion of an encompassing divine sanction for human decisions based on contingency and creativity. Sinai revelation thus becomes an overwhelming religious category blanketing any human innovative mode.

At the same time, it was in yeshiva that I absorbed the axiom of *yeridat ha-dorot* (generational decline), that only earlier generations had it truly right. The further we move from Sinai in history, the weaker our potential access to divine truth. It naturally followed that precedents set by earlier generations anchored our dominant frame of reference. The past was sacrosanct, and the future, by extension, was ever suspect. Within this mind-set, the past was truly, as the saying goes, never past—indeed, its insistent presence as ultimate arbiter of value for the living community eclipsed the possibility of drawing much meaning or inspiration from the future. The future was not a source of optimism, a harbinger of potential progress, but rather something errant and threatening, always in need of being anchored and re-anchored into the primordial moment of revelation, and, finally, somehow integrated into the tradition in which that revelation is lived.

Within this worldview, the notion of a collective growth in knowledge and wisdom with the unfolding of historical experience was given no place. This radical contemporaneity, the eternal presence of the past, also leads to the rejection of any notion that earlier, received thought has a historical context. The contextualization of Rabbinic thinking with respect to social factors and cultural influences is totally alien to the yeshiva learning spirit. Such an intrusion might risk making received tradition seem less immediate, the very opposite of what we were striving to accomplish. Everything on the page of the Talmud is considered contemporary. It is not important when or where the Talmudic text was written (third- to fifth-century Babylonia), or when or where Rashi, its most authoritative interpreter whose commentary sits adjacent to it on the Talmudic page, lived and thought and wrote (twelfth-century Provence, as it happens), or what the mores of his culture dictated, much less how he might have been impacted by them. History, for the yeshiva, has no epistemology, and certainly no effect on the minds of rabbis or the content of Torah.

In my thirties I remained a yeshiva *bachur* while working as a newly minted pulpit rabbi. In that role, my great communal spiritual challenges revolved around pushing my congregation toward greater and stricter observance of mitzvot. Can I convince the mourner to overcome personal or social awkwardness and tear his or her clothes in earnest, fulfilling the halakhic requirement of *keria* to the fullest extent? Can I convince a struggling shul to devote time and resources to building a *mehitza* (synagogue gender-separation barrier)—separation of the sexes being a major religious concern of the Orthodox establishment? My success at this latter endeavor was considered a major achievement and source of inspiration among my rabbinic mentors and peers. *Hartman took a mixed-pew congregation and separated it!* Suddenly I was a hero of the yeshiva world. *Orthodoxy can be victorious!* I felt like King David battling the assimilatory Goliath. Many of these battles seemed to take place around life-cycle ceremonies, times in which the less observant often turn to Orthodox religious authorities for ritual guidance. Could I persuade the mourning family not to leave the cemetery until the casket has been sufficiently (according to the halakhic standard) covered with dirt?

In the midst of my attempt at staging an Orthodox religious revival, it did not often occur to me to notice that my synagogue was largely empty, much less to ask why. There would be times when the reality of its emptiness would hit me, but the imperative of influencing other Jews to greater observance was so serious and engrossing, so pressing and ever present, that deeper spiritual and intellectual issues could easily be avoided. *What is the real significance of all this?* and *What are the ethical implications of this lifestyle?* were questions I never asked. The only real ethical issues I can recall facing at this time were on the order of: How can I give a mournful *hesped* (eulogy) when I did not personally know the deceased? How can I make sure the things I say are true, that my language does not meander into a rhetoric of falseness and flattery, but instead attempts humbly to mirror the reality of the mourners and of the dead?

While meaningful on its own terms, this was essentially an ethics of self. Neither the social-political issues of the larger society (for example, the struggle for civil rights) nor even of the broader Jewish world (the delegitimization and dehumanization of non-Orthodox rabbis and Jews) registered in my consciousness, much less touched my conscience, at that time. To the contrary, I understood how dangerous it was to allow the Conservative movement to thrive and believed that the future of Judaism would be destroyed by these alien rabbis who had not studied within, and did not affirm the axioms of, the history-transcending yeshiva ethos. It was precisely when they began to speak about the tradition within its historical contexts that these rabbis became most threatening, for it was this perspective of historical distance that disqualified them as authentic carriers of the Jewish story. Their willingness to contextualize that story using the tools of history, sociology, philosophy, and psychology proved they were outside the pale of the normal, accepted way of Jewish learning and knowing sanctified by hundreds of years of students studying Torah in a specific way.

Thus, while relentless analytical questioning forms the intellectual backbone of Talmud study, the overall frame of reference, the system as a whole, is not questioned. To the contrary, such second-order questioning, or anything that might lead to it, is discouraged and, if raised, squelched. I recall a moment from my time as a student in Lakewood Yeshiva, the flagship institution of Lithuanian ultra-Orthodox learning in America, where my passion for Torah study first truly took hold. I was reading a popular Torah commentary written by Rabbi Joseph Hertz, a former chief rabbi of England, whose glosses often drew upon non-Jewish scholars to shed light on the biblical text. While I was reading, an older yeshiva boy came by, took note of the author, grabbed the book out of my hand, and threw it on the floor. "*Treyfus!*" he declared, using the Yiddish for "nonkosher." There was no room for discussion; to him the admixture of history and Torah was vulgar and had no place in the holy *mesorah*, in the sanctuaries and study halls of legitimate Jewish discourse.

The well-ordered system throughout my learning period was shot through with moments of uncertainty. In the silence of myself I began to feel unsettled. I had a growing sense that these "alien" perspectives should be confronted—that they were relevant, perhaps even necessary, for a true and full understanding of the tradition and its development throughout history and across cultures. This shift did not arise out of a rebellious spirit, but out of love: I loved the Torah so much that I wanted to understand it as thoroughly as possible. The question of why these external ideas needed to be stigmatized as threatening began to nag at me. In part, this hypervigilance seemed to bespeak a deep sense of insecurity on the part of Orthodox leadership. Why must we close off the rest of the world in order to feel secure in our own?

My decision to leave Lakewood for Yeshiva University was motivated largely by dissatisfaction with the intellectual insularity I had come to associate with the ultra-Orthodox yeshiva world. Yeshiva University, with the bold commitment to intellectual openness announced in its credo, *Torah u-Mada* (lit. "Torah and Secular Knowledge"), promised a broadening of horizons. This promise was realized in the person of Rabbi Joseph B. Soloveitchik, the great theologian of modern Orthodoxy. Renowned for his sophisticated, erudite integration of halakhic thinking and Western philosophy, "the Rav" became my teacher and mentor. I was a devoted student, thrilled by his sheer intellectual vigor as he quoted Christian existentialists—Søren Kierkegaard, Rudolph Otto—in the same breath as Talmudic luminaries from across the generations. It was Rabbi Soloveitchik who urged me to go to graduate school in philosophy, and it was then that my world began to undergo a major change.

My first real break with an intense yeshiva mind-set occurred when I was doing graduate work in philosophy at Fordham University. Among the Jesuit community there, I encountered a very deep religious integrity that challenged many of the assumptions about non-Jewish people and religions I had been taught to consider immutable facts of nature. I often found myself being spiritually inspired by people who came out of traditions I had learned to think of as valueless, tainted, *treyf*. Meanwhile, in the course of commuting between Fordham and Yeshiva, I was often struck by an awareness that my Catholic philosophy instructors were inspiring far more religious connection and consciousness than my rabbis at Yeshiva. How might such experiences impact my understanding and practice of traditional Judaism? How did they relate to the many sections of the Talmud that exhibit harsh, negative attitudes toward non-Jews and codify these attitudes into diminished ethical responsibilities?

At Fordham I had the privilege of meeting Professor Robert C. Pollack, a great religious and intellectual spirit who engaged me with a unique perspective on Spinoza and forced me to rethink the Spinozan challenge to traditional Judaism. His experiential way of doing philosophy provided a powerful introduction for me to the school of American Pragmatism—above all, through John Dewey and William James. This compelling mode of relating to ideas forced me to ask myself, *What difference do ideas make in experience?* and to look at the world of experience as a way of clarifying the meaning of ideas. Through Pollack, I became anchored deeply in the significance of lived reality, rather than metaphysical speculation, as a critical factor in the honest assessment of theological claims.

Once the walls of the yeshiva had begun to break down, other philosophical trends began to impact on my thinking. John Stewart Mill and Isaiah Berlin became significant figures in my spiritual life. Mill forced me to grapple with notions of individual autonomy absent from or downplayed within the yeshiva world. I was very moved by Berlin's understanding of history and the development of ideas. His highly original analysis of the nineteenth century, his conception of liberty—these were things that occupied my mind and brought a sense of fresh air to my thinking. I recall the intense desire during those years to read everything he wrote.

At Fordham, I also encountered for the first time scholars of religion who spoke of disagreements between Maimonides and other rabbinic commentators as having a historical and social context. I came to understand that without a grasp of the worlds of Christian and Muslim Europe out of which these commentators emerged, it was impossible to fully understand their interpretations and halakhic verdicts. The neat barriers erected by formalistic Talmudic analysis began to buckle with my discovery of history. While studying the classical sources, I began to wonder: What did Rome look like? What did the people look like who lived there? Who was the woman? Who was the pagan? To the secular academic mind these questions may sound obvious, even naïve; given my background, they came as a revelation. Suddenly, the yeshiva boy had taken the closed books of the New Testament and the church fathers and begun to contemplate their world, all in the service of his passion for Talmudic clarity.

Notwithstanding my intentions, this exploration was considered heresy by my former teachers and peers, an abandonment of the tradition's axiomatic self-sufficiency. Nevertheless, it resonated in my soul. When the edifice of my yeshiva worldview began to crack and shift, what emerged was a personal quest for a frame of reference that would enable me to remain within the tradition, yet at the same time recognize its inadequacies and incompleteness. Embracing this intellectual path, encountering so many significant individuals with so much to say about the meaning of life and what elements enter into the creation of an identity, altered my perspective on the Torah world that I loved so much. Suddenly, new issues began to surface. My Judaism had to face the criticism of Mordecai Kaplan and William James, of contemporary thinkers like Peter Berger and Charles Taylor. My *beit midrash* had new students and new teachers. I could no longer hide between the coattails of my erstwhile rebbes and *rosh yeshivas* (the academic heads of yeshivas), who insisted that the received system was perfect and any introduction of alien thought misplaced and dangerous, taboo.

When I was going through my exposure to nontraditional sources of knowledge, wondering where I would land, how much of what I was taught to believe and experience I could continue with, I was lost but still deeply in love with Judaism and the Jewish people. Initially, my most significant moral conflict with Jewish tradition centered around its treatment of the non-Jew, which I came to feel was fundamentally wrong. The weakening of the system was mediated by its reflexively suspicious and hostile attitude toward the "other."

Later, the gender issue broke into my consciousness as my daughter Tova began challenging the role of women in the synagogue. Her intensity never wavered, and it was impossible for me to ignore the issues of gender within the tradition while she was fighting, writing, and building. A persistent, committed, and sharply insightful evaluation of how these issues were treated by much of the halakhic and Orthodox theological world revealed to me how inadequate the tradition had been in dealing with such a fundamental challenge. I became unable to justify women's exclusion from a minyan; why should they be denied the religious dignity that comes with full communal partic-ipation, treated, in essence, as if they were not there? I could not understand a world in which a woman might function as an active, cre-ative person in law or medicine, for example—a person in whom peo-ple would place their trust and, in some circumstances, their lives—and then, the moment she leaves the hospital or the courtroom and enters the synagogue, become transformed into a nonperson, with many of the same status limitations as a child or a slave. The dehuman-izing tendency of the halakhic treatment of women further opened the crack in my religious allegiance to the traditional faith-articles of Orthodoxy.

Eventually I came to understand that Tova was not merely fight-ing for women's rights, but for an honest, authentic Judaism. She helped me to see that the issue is not fundamentally about "women's rights," but about the type of God I worship. Could I worship a God who considered half of the Jewish community to be not fully human and responsible? She showed me, finally, the ways in which my male-dominated religion was shot through with deep immoralities. I could no longer hide within the four-cubits of halakha, no matter how com-fortable, energizing, and inspiring that life might often be.

The ultimate challenge to my religious worldview came as I embraced, totally, the emergence of the Israeli reality. I was convinced that Israel represented the potential for a profound renaissance, a rethinking of Jewish values such as attitudes toward the *ger* (non-Jew/stranger). My emerging perspectives on the nonobservant Jew and on the significance of the secular world began to claim me in a very sharp and existential way. My experience with the world of the Orthodox community in Israel brought me to recognize what type of limited human being grows from a tradition that is not exposed to alternative perspectives.

I found myself now completely isolated, intellectually, from the Talmudic academies in which I had grown up, from the religious lead-ers who studiously and self-righteously ignored the compelling cri-tiques that the modern world presents to traditional Judaism. That community—with its failure even to attempt to lead the members of the new Jewish state into a higher moral stance, a more serious encounter with God and the mitzvot; with its overwhelming emphasis on sexual modesty, kashrut, and a host of miscellaneous trivia, as the ultimate carriers of authentic Judaism—simply lost any significance for me. I was repulsed by its authoritarian, dogmatic thinking and its refusal to encounter alternative spiritual and intellectual traditions with the potential to cast a different light on the meaning of being a committed Jew.

Nevertheless, it is in Israel that I found, and continue to seek, community: others who want to be engaged by a compelling spiritual reality that mirrors and enhances the realities of lived life, rejecting the ever-tempting escape into authoritative symbolism; others who are spiritually bored, yet remain claimed by a tradition much of which does not speak to them anymore. In Israel I came to realize that my loneliness was not unique, that there were many Israelis experiencing their own version of this strange mixture of commitment and alienation. I found others eager to join me in the critical reflection of Judaism's encounter with modernity.

Eventually, as I mentioned above, I founded an institution to house this unfolding endeavor. It was at the Shalom Hartman Institute that I was able to find and collect people with great minds and great honesty, uninterested in hiding in a verbal, metaphysical religion disconnected from their daily experience of life. There I have been provided with the moral nourishment of a living dialogue with people who have intellectual courage and respect for alternative ways of life and thinking. Many seem to find it a refuge of intellectual freedom; no one is attacked or criticized for thinking in new ways. The institute became my spiritual home, in which I met fellow truth seekers who were able to live with uncertainty and doubt.

On Being Human and a Jew

In a sense, this book is an attempt to articulate some of the insights acquired over the course of this journey, as my comfortable four-cubits of halakha began to expand and demand the inclusion of any human insight that can shed light on what it means to be a human being and a Jew. I am still in the process of searching. People sometimes ask me, have you decided what you want to do when you grow up? My answer is, I don't know. I don't know where I am going to land, but this book maps the road on which I continue to travel. I only hope to continue to find new insights into Judaism, which in turn continue to nourish me within the halakhic tradition.

A final note: Some of my critiques of the halakhic system may mirror critiques that have been made by non-Orthodox Jewish denominations. If the reader finds such similarities, these are choruses I am happy to join. Personally, I remain deeply appreciative of the traditional framework of the home I grew up in and the schools in which I studied. *Hakarat ha-tov*, acknowledgment and appreciation, is an important Jewish value, and my appreciation to the world of my upbringing cannot be overstated, and my foundational memories—of my parents' and brothers' dedication to Torah and to helping other Jews; the ambience of Brownsville, New York; the *shtiebl* I grew up in; the intensity of Lakewood Yeshiva—remain live reservoirs of joy for me, both in the memories they imprinted on my consciousness and in the ways in which they stamped my sensibilities.

The same type of boundless, eternal *hakarat ha-tov* applies to Rabbi Soloveitchik. Even as I have come to part company with much of his teaching, my love and appreciation of him, and of the world of halakha-philosophy to which he so beautifully and powerfully introduced me, remain firmly in place. It was he who sent me the decisive letter of recommendation to Fordham University, pushing me not only to study philosophy, but to study it *away* from Yeshiva, where it could not be held prisoner to Orthodox dogma.

Finally, when I think of the foundational memories that shaped my life religiously, I cannot ignore the joyful influence of my beloved friend Shlomo Carlebach. His music set me on fire, and that fire has never been extinguished.

It is my hope that this book will help the reader to appreciate something of the complexity of religious life as I experience it and the type of struggle that constitutes an important feature of my everyday teaching and learning. *Yismach lev mevakshei Hashem*, "Let all who *seek* the Lord rejoice" (Ps. 105:3; emphasis added). Anyone curious about the Jewish way of life, yet dissatisfied with much of contemporary Jewish theology and practice—repelled, perhaps, by the cheap and vulgar apologetics of those who seek to justify and sustain some of the tradition's systematic immoralities, who smugly deny expression to any doubt or uncertainty, claiming a monopoly on absolute truth—is invited to join me on this pilgrimage.

1

HALAKHIC SPIRITUALITY
Living in the Presence of God

The moral and theological issues that emerge from the situations described in the Introduction would, for the most part, disappear if halakha (Jewish law) did not command such centrality within Jewish tradition. Given that these kinds of issues seem to be, if not endemic to the halakhic system, quite prevalent within it, it would certainly be reasonable to ask: Why do I consider halakha so important? What is its deep significance? In spite of all these issues, why do I find it so central, and how do I understand my commitment to it? I should say first that questions about the grounds for halakhic authority have never held much interest for me. I can say categorically that I have no interest in rehabilitating or defending the theological principles that are used to fortify its presumptive authority. I grapple with halakha's significance, rather, intellectually, spiritually, and experientially, because of its centrality to my historical family. I grapple with it because I am claimed—at times inspired, at times haunted, but always claimed—by the question of why it has occupied such a formidable role within Jewish life, its central role in shaping the religious character of the Jewish people.

It is perhaps revealing to consider that my interest in discovering the meanings halakha held for my grandparents, and their grandparents, mirrors, in an interesting way, the basis for its widespread indifference among contemporary Jews. Just as my commitment does not derive from halakha's authority, neither does their indifference derive from a rejection of its authority. Authority, for most modern Jews, is simply a dead-letter issue. Halakha is not rejected because modern, enlightened Jews reject the theological premise that it was given by God. They never get to the point of asking questions about its origins, dismissing it long before such questions might arise because of the difficulty of finding God in the lifestyle it seems to cultivate and obligate. Indifference to halakha most commonly derives from an inability of most Jews to find religious value within the system. As Abraham Joshua Heschel, twentieth-century Judaism's great poet-theologian, correctly claimed:

> A serious difficulty is the problem of the meaning of Jewish observance. The modern Jew cannot accept the way of static obedience as a short cut to the mystery of the divine will. His religious situation is not conducive to an attitude of intellectual or spiritual surrender. He is not ready to sacrifice his liberty on the altar of loyalty to the spirit of the ancestors. He will only respond to a demonstration that there is meaning to be found in what is expected of him. *His primary difficulty is not in his inability to comprehend the divine origin of the law; his essential difficulty is in his ability to sense the presence of divine meaning in the fulfillment of the law.* [emphasis added][1]

My own familiarity with modern Jews' halakhic indifference, drawing on a plethora of firsthand experience stretching back decades, confirms Heschel's observation. While training to be a rabbi at Yeshiva University, halakha was my entire life. I studied many sections of the *Shulchan Arukh*, the bedrock text of Jewish law, relating to questions of kashrut and other extensive and technically intricate areas of Jewish law. This was all in preparation to function as a competent, well-informed rabbi, a large part of whose duties would, I expected, involve responding to the halakhic questions posed by members of my community.

I vividly recall the first few years in my pulpit, waiting eagerly for such questions to arise. While there was no shortage of work to be done, a part of me nonetheless yearned to employ the extensive training I had received, to gain experience in that dimension of the rabbinate. To my surprise, and chagrin, not one halakhic question was raised.

Then one day I was in a cemetery performing an unveiling for one of my congregants, and a woman approached me with a heavy bearing and a solemn look on her face. "Rabbi," she said, "I have a very important question to ask you. But I see that you are very young, and perhaps this question is meant for someone who has already served many years in the rabbinate." I urged her to share her question with me, reassuring her that if it proved too difficult for me to answer, I would be honest and refer her to a more senior rabbi. She asked me, "Can I light a *yahrzeit* lamp [a ceremonial flame used to commemorate a parent's death] for my mother?" "What's the problem?" I responded. I had been well-trained in the area of halakha relating to death and mourning, so I felt confident that I would be able to help her. A *yahrzeit* lamp would certainly be the appropriate response to a deceased parent. "You see," she continued, "I light a *yahrzeit* lamp for my father, and I wanted to have a *yahrzeit* lamp for my mother, since they loved each other all their lives, and I know they are still very close." I listened sincerely. I felt for this woman who had lost her parents and seemed haunted and distressed over the loss. Still, as closely as I listened, I was not able to discern the halakhic question for which she sought resolution. Perhaps my inexperience was showing through after all. "Miss, I would very much like to help you," I said. "What is the problem?" "Well," she explained, "you see, my mother is still alive. I just wanted them to be next to each other in the candles I light."

I mustered a serious face, seeing how important the question seemed to this woman. I told her it was a very difficult question, gave her my phone number and asked her to call me back in a week or so in order that I might have time to research thoroughly, contemplate seriously, and ultimately provide her with an authoritative, meaningful answer. But I left the cemetery depressed. The first halakhic question I ever received as a rabbi had proved to be, from a strictly halakhic perspective, absurd. This simple story is relatively typical of the interest in halakha I encountered throughout my early years in the rabbinate. I soon realized that my halakhic training had been totally in vain.

In another example told to me by a rabbinic colleague, a congregant approached him with what he presented as a very urgent halakhic question. The congregant wanted to know if he could sit *shiva* (the week of mourning and consolation directly following burial of a first-degree relative, the traditional observance of which involves abstaining from work) for his father. My colleague could not discern the halakhic conflict. Sitting *shiva* for his father would have been not a choice but an obligation. Why *wouldn't* he do it? "Well, rabbi," he explained, "my father is not dead yet. He's dying, but he's not dead." This gentleman wanted to know if it would be possible to find a halakhic precedent that would allow him to get the *shiva* out of the way early, as the business season was about to begin and he did not want to have to suffer the economic loss of missing work.

These are the questions rabbis receive even in somewhat *traditional* Jewish environments. Today, all the more so, there is little vestige found of the type of concern with halakha that was once prevalent within Jewish communities. Outside of a small slice of the contemporary Jewish world, the irrelevance of halakha is nearly total. Who is really bothered by such questions? Many contemporary Jews find it less problematic to embrace midrashic-haggadic (narrative-philosophical) texts as an access point for encountering the tradition. Talmudic legalisms, elaborate discussions on the minutia of Jewish law, do not appear to evoke much enthusiasm on the part of most Jews. Granted, the ultra-Orthodox Hassidic and yeshiva communities take halakhic questions very seriously, and the latter in particular is a world I was raised in and nurtured by, as I discussed in the Introduction. It is also, however, a world I long ago left to find a more eclectic and critical path within the Jewish tradition. Thus the question still naggingly remains: why do I take halakha seriously?

And so, before confronting the dilemmas raised in the Introduction, I find it important to explore and explain why I feel that halakha still stands as a potentially valuable and compelling spiritual option for the Jewish people. What has goaded me personally into a lifelong engagement with halakha is the challenge to provide a coherent understanding of the lifestyle it framed and held for the generations upon generations who lived it before me. It is a lifestyle marked by a great prevalence of legal details aspiring to address every aspect of human experience. How do I grasp the meaning of this system's enormous scope? (As a vivid example of this consuming aspiration, I recall that Young Israel, a movement of synagogues within modern American Orthodoxy, used to offer courses called "From the Cradle to the Grave," emphasizing the encompassing range of life experiences, from marriage to sex to work to war, permeated by halakhic questions and answers.) How do I grasp the historical fact that the Jewish people were, for so many centuries, a halakhic people?

While the origins of halakha are to be found within the biblical mitzvot, the dynamic religious focus of the Bible is clearly the God of history and this God's erratic, hot-and-cold relationship with His "kingdom of priests," His "holy people." This powerful strain of religious thinking, emphasizing the imminent, interventionist God, punishing and rewarding according to our deeds, was taken up powerfully by a prominent strain of rabbinic thinking. One of its most potent and influential expressions is found in the work of the medieval Spanish rabbi, poet, and philosopher Yehuda Halevi. According to Halevi, it is historical events that mediate the reality of God for the Jewish people. In this respect he saw his own generation as no different from their biblical forebears, interpreting God's will and God's mood through its expression in the rise and fall of Jewish fortunes.

God-Consciousness: Finding God's Love in His Silence

Maimonides, the medieval rabbi dually distinguished as Jewish tradition's greatest halakhist and philosopher, viewed God's relationship to the Jewish people in an entirely different light. For him, history held little if any significance from a religious perspective. God was encountered not through miracle, not through historical events, but through individual philosophical contemplation upon

God's created world. This contemplation led to the philosophical love of God that for Maimonides represents the height of human spiritual achievement.

Upon what basis did Maimonides overturn the biblical paradigm and exit history as the central Jewish religious field of meaning? As I have demonstrated at length elsewhere,[2] Maimonides picks up on a motif of Rabbinic theology found throughout the Talmud that acknowledges the defeat of the concept of an interventionist, historical God as a live spiritual option for the Jewish people. With the destruction of the First Temple and the Babylonian Exile (c. 586 BCE), Jews faced the trauma of attempting to understand the role of God—a God who appears to have abandoned them to the whims of other rulers, to servitude, forced wandering, and slaughter—in the life of His elected nation.

> Rabbi Yehoshua ben Levi said: Why were they called the Men of the "Great" Assembly? Because they restored the crown of the divine attributes to its ancient completeness [i.e., brought about a renewal of God's "greatness"]. Moses came and said: "The great, powerful, and awesome God." Jeremiah [who prophesied during the destruction of the First Temple] followed and said: Strangers are frolicking in His sanctuary! Where are the displays of His "awesomeness"? Therefore he omitted "awesome" [i.e., he removed it from his prayer]. Daniel [who lived during the Babylonian Captivity that followed the First Temple's destruction] followed and said: Strangers are enslaving His children! Where are the displays of His "power"? And so he did not say "powerful" in his prayer. [The Men of the Great Assembly] followed and said: On the contrary! This is His magnificent strength, for He restrains His will, showing forbearance to the wicked. And these are the displays of His "awesomeness": because, were it not for the awe [i.e., of the nations] of the Holy One, blessed be He, how could one solitary, singular nation survive among the nations of the world?
>
> (BT YOMA 69B)

Moses, who is the authority for the correct notion of divine power as well as for the normative behavior of the community, had described God in prayer as "great ... mighty, and ... awesome" (Deut. 10:17). In the biblical context, "mighty and awesome" refers to God's victorious power in history, which enables a prophet to defeat a Pharaoh, but Jeremiah and Daniel's experience of history did not correspond to the portrait of God's power depicted by Moses. This is how the Talmud explains why in their prayers we find God addressed only as "great and mighty" (Jer. 32:18) and "great and awesome" (Dan. 9:4). When they were unable to see God's might or awesomeness, they did not want to "ascribe false things to Him" (BT *Yoma* 69b). The Men of the Great Assembly, on the other hand, demonstrated *their* greatness by finding a way of restoring the full Mosaic formula when they offered prayer at the renewal of the Sinai covenant. They were able to recognize the might and awesomeness of God in His ability to restrain Himself and not wrathfully strike down the oppressors of Israel.

It is a key point within this story that for the Rabbis, it was the reality of history that shaped their conception of religious language. Truth must grow out of their lived experience, not claims of truth based on authority. They could not use a language that they would know in their hearts was false or meaningless, calling self-deception in a matter of such religious import "ascribing falsehood to God." The lived experience of the community must be the validation of their religious language.

What we have, then, is on one hand a commitment to Moses's language and on the other a necessity to rethink its meaning. This language must be understood in a new way if we are to use it in prayer. Here we find the Rabbis boldly asserting that the tradition can claim you only if it is mirrored truthfully in the world you live in. Tradition could live not through its claims of absolute truth based on revelation, but on the lived reality of the Jewish people's experience of that truth. The tradition *becomes* true if it remains a plausible description of the world they live in. The implications of this approach have great resonance for modern Jews who want to be honest and truthful and loyal to the tradition and yet find themselves bothered that they don't find the implications of the religious language of the tradition mirrored in their experience.

In these texts, then, we find the Talmudic Rabbis—in the face of God's apparent defeat and indifference, finding themselves no longer able to experience history authentically within the biblical paradigm of His military leadership of a triumphant Jewish nation—alive to this challenge, searching their language to affirm the presence of a loving, providential God in a world of war and exile. The experience of God's silence required explanation in light of the inherited paradigms of the Exodus from Egypt. In the Passover story, God facilitates a total redemption experience for the Jews. Yet in times closer to the Rabbis' experience, Israel is defeated brutally, its people slaughtered and exiled, its Temples destroyed, first by Babylonia, then Rome. *Where are You, God?* was a question deeply felt within the soul of the Jewish nation. If the great drama and vitality of their story were to continue, it would be necessary to find a new way of mediating their relationship with God. Unable to exalt in God's victories, they were nevertheless able to maintain their loyalty to Him because they could perceive His power also in His acceptance of defeat.

A similar expression of this motif is found in the midst of a Talmudic narrative describing the destruction of the Second Temple:

> Abba Chanan says: "Who is like You, O Strong One, God?" (Ps. 89:9)—Who is like You, strong and firm, for You hear the insult and blasphemy of the evil, yet remain silent? In the academy of Rabbi Yishmael it was taught: "Who is like You among the mighty ones [*eilim*], God?" (Exod. 15:11)—Who is like You among the silent ones [*ilmim*]?
>
> (BT *GITTIN* 56B)

These texts clearly reveal a people fully aware of God's indifference to the suffering condition and humiliation of the Jews in history. Here, too, we find that this acute awareness led them not to a Nietzschean death-of-God theology, but rather to a rethinking of the biblical descriptions of God as all-powerful (*gibor*).[3]

The reality of history gives rise to a new theology of divine power, a new stage of the covenantal relationship: divine omnipotence leads not to an expectation of Israel's victorious triumph over its enemies, but rather to an appreciation of God's love in His silence. In witnessing Israel's humiliation, God remains silent to give the evil powers in history the opportunity to go through repentance, waiting silently for evil men to find their way back to their true humanity. Divine restraint is the new understanding of divine power.

With this total, radical neutralization of the biblical Lord of history, the question naturally arises: where *can* a living God be found? For the Talmudic Sages, it was halakha that replaced history as the new medium within which to encounter the living reality of God. "After the destruction of the [Second] Temple, God is, in His world, only within the four cubits of halakha" (BT *Berachot* 8a). The positive significance of observing the mitzvot for Jews can potentially outweigh their experienced misfortunes. When instant successes against idolatrous enemies are no longer a criterion for perceiving the active presence of God, that presence can be felt all the more strongly in the day-to-day observances and practices of Judaism. The living God is experienced in the rich variety of opportunities to connect every life activity to consciousness of mitzvah. In the Talmud, the biblical mitzvot are exhaustively explicated and elaborated, analyzed and amplified, until their reach expands to address virtually every corner of human experience. As all mitzvot recall the original mitzvah, the covenantal call at Sinai—God's desire for a relationship with the Jewish people and sealing of that relationship through an experience of revelatory intimacy, extended through history by fidelity to its code of behavior and ritual—the effect of their amplification through the halakhic process is, at least ideally, to create a community saturated with awareness of the Divine in every aspect of its individual and collective life.

Within this Rabbinic thread, it is Torah that now incarnates the living God of history. God remains incarnate in history by the fact that God's Torah is present within the life of the community. The study of Torah, with its infinite unfolding of interpretive possibilities, offers an experience of the richness of the living God. Halakha, then, is far more than pure legalism. For proof, we need look no further than traditional yeshiva students, rocking and singing as they learn, as if study were an act of total worship. Psalm 119 gives expression to this religious mood in which Torah, and the way of life it shapes, is now seen as manifesting God's presence in history:

> *I have turned to You with all my heart;*
> *do not let me stray from Your commandments. (v.10)*
> *I am racked with grief;*
> *sustain me in accordance with Your word. (v.28)*
> *I shall have an answer for those who taunt me,*
> *for I have put my trust in Your word. (v.42)*
> *Do not utterly take the truth away from my mouth,*
> *for I have put my hope in Your rules. (v.43)*
> *Teach me good sense and knowledge,*
> *for I have put my trust in Your commandments. (v.66)*
> *Those who fear You will see me and rejoice,*
> *for I have put my hope in Your word. (v.74)*
> *May Your mercy reach me, that I might live,*
> *for Your teaching is my delight. (v.77)*
> *I long for Your deliverance;*
> *I hope for Your word. (v.81)*
> *I will never neglect Your precepts,*
> *for You have preserved my life through them. (v.93)*
> *I am Yours; save me!*
> *For I have turned to Your precepts. (v.94)*
> *My flesh creeps from fear of You;*
> *I am in awe of Your rulings. (v.120)*
> *I rise before dawn and cry for help;*
> *I hope for Your word. (v.147)*

According to the letter and spirit of this text, the word of God is interchangeable with God. Torah, therefore, conveys the immediacy of God's presence, as if it were an incarnation of God's will and love.

The Role of Halakha in God-Intoxication

For the Rabbis, then, the great potential of halakha lies in its power to create a life intoxicated by the consciousness of God. "Let all your actions be for the sake of heaven" (*Pirkei Avot* 2:12); "In all your ways: know Him" (Prov. 3:6); "I am ever mindful of the Lord's presence" (Ps. 16:8): these biblical and Talmudic imperatives express the impulse that created the halakha. The Rabbis gathered these threads of Judaic thinking and wove them into a new mediating principle for the Divine, one powerful enough to replace the absence of God's miraculous involvement in history. By finally acknowledging defeat in that hopeless, depleted sphere, they circumscribed a new area of religious aspiration. God would no longer be found in miraculous intervention, but in the materials of everyday human life. It is for this reason that the Talmudic Rabbis, and their successors, so tirelessly dedicated themselves to finding new opportunities to tie mitzvot to daily activity. We fill our lives with mitzvah in order to cultivate the habit of mind that we live within the encompassing presence of God. This is what I mean by my claim that a founding impulse and intended effect of halakha is God-intoxication.

It has been my claim that the turn from history as a focus of religious meaning, found within this strain of Rabbinic theology, supplied a precedent that Maimonides then appropriated into his deeply philosophical understanding of religious life. For him, neither history nor halakha mediates the deepest encounter with the Divine, but rather the philosophical love of God. It was Maimonides's deep knowledge of Talmud that allowed him this opportunity to appropriate the metaphysical God of Aristotle within Judaism; the Bible alone would have made it impossible to create such a thorough integration of Greek philosophy. It was the Talmudic neutralization of divine power within history that enabled him to fall in love with Aristotle's god.

For Maimonides, halakha plays an important, but secondary, role in the religious process; its function is to create the conditions of individual and societal character optimal for making such a love relationship possible. Thus, the mitzvot as expressed in halakha are still critical in the service of God. He places them in a similar category to the kinds of physical and moral self-maintenance necessary for a strong, healthy physical and spiritual personality—the type of personality that might become capable of essaying the summits of philosophical contemplation of the Divine. In a sense, Maimonides takes the God-intoxicated impulse expressed by the Talmud through halakhic analysis and expansion and expands it further to include areas of life those Rabbis left halakhically neutral.

> *A person should intend each and every one of his actions exclusively toward knowing God, blessed be He.* His sitting and rising, and his speech, everything: toward this one goal. For example: when he does business, or works for pay, his intent should be not only for the accumulation of money, but in order to find things the body needs, from eating to drinking, to establishing a home, to marrying. Moreover, when a person does eat and drink and have sex, he should not intend to do these things for pleasure alone, until he only eats and drinks what is sweet to taste, and has sex exclusively for physical pleasure, like a dog or a mule. Rather, a person should eat things that contribute to health and well-being, whether bitter or sweet. Nor should he eat things that are harmful to the body, sweet though they may be.... Furthermore, to conduct himself exclusively according to the principles of physical well-being—if his intent is only that his body and limbs will be whole and strong, so that he may have children who do his bidding and toil on his behalf— this is still not a good path. Rather, let him intend for his body to be whole and strong, so as to endow his soul with the integrity to know God. For it is impossible to understand or to delve into the fields of wisdom when a person is sick or in pain.... It emerges that a person who walks in this path his entire life worships God always, even while doing business, even while having sex—because in all of this, his intent is to gather the resources such that his body is wholly prepared for the worship of God. And thus even in the hours when such a

person is sleeping, if he is sleeping in order to rest his mind, in order that his body does not get sick, which would make him unable to worship God: we find that this sleep constitutes worship of God. *And in this matter the Sages commanded and said, "Let all your actions be for the sake of heaven." And this is what King Solomon said, in his wisdom: "In all your ways, know Him,"* (Prov. 3:6). [emphasis added][4]

For Maimonides, God-intoxication is achieved by using the power of conscious intent to enlist all of our faculties and actions in the service of the philosophical contemplation of God. He says elsewhere that halakha functions in a similar way. As we harness greater and greater aspects of ourselves toward this lofty and elusive goal—the only goal worthy, in his thinking, of the potential with which God imbued humanity, and the true end goal of His covenant with the Jewish people at Sinai—we sanctify our lives with a sense of holy purpose. The well-known proverb "In all your ways, know Him" (Prov. 3:6) is understood by Maimonides to mean something like, "Let all your ways be directed toward bringing you ever closer to the possibility of encountering Him through philosophical contemplation."

Maimonides clearly is interested in cultivating a religious personality who is always thinking about God. And while the Talmudic turn from history provides a substantive precedent for his ahistorical theology, there also is an important distinction to be drawn between his version of God-intoxication and that espoused by the Talmudic Sages. For Maimonides, halakha is, to be sure, a site of spiritual significance; still, its value is ultimately instrumental. It is the framework that sets the stage, as it were, for the intellectual love of God. He states this explicitly in the philosophical introductory chapter to his halakhic opus, the *Mishneh Torah*. In reference to "the clarification of what is prohibited versus permissible, and all related matters among the other mitzvot," he points out that the Talmudic Sages themselves referred to this dimension of religious concern as a "small thing" relative to the religious weight to which they assigned, he claims, philosophical knowledge of God. Nevertheless, he endorses halakha as appropriate preparation and training for this ultimate objective, for obtaining clarity in matters of halakha, as in other areas of uncertainty, "settles a person's mind" (*Yesodei Ha-Torah* 4:18). Halakha is about personal character development and developing the political conditions prerequisite to the love of God. Maimonides understood its instrumental value for community inasmuch as it creates an ordered, psychologically and physically healthy person. Moreover, he understood halakha made this level of spiritual achievement accessible to the masses. But it is nothing like the ultimate goal of the religious quest.

This limitation presents no problem for Maimonides, as such an experience is neither halakha's purpose nor its purview. Maimonides makes this point explicit near the end of the *Guide for the Perplexed*, asserting that even the greatest halakhists:

> believe true opinions on the basis of traditional authority and study the law concerning the practices of divine service, but do not engage in speculation concerning the fundamental principles of religion and make no inquiry whatever regarding the rectification of belief.[5]

But the halakhists never achieve a direct experience of God. Within his worldview, the intellect is the ultimate channel of divine encounter, leaving room for only one truly God-intoxicated figure: the philosopher.

Judaism: Building a Community Suffused with God-Consciousness

As I have written elsewhere, I am in full agreement with a central religious impulse found in these Maimonidean texts, the turn from history toward a theology of consuming God-consciousness. I depart from him, however, in placing the ultimate religious ideal exclusively within the sphere of a philosophical love relationship mediated entirely by intellectual perfection. In this, I believe my view is closer to the spirit of the Talmud. It also makes me sympathetic to the indignant criticism of Maimonides's work. In his anthology of the laws pertaining to the mitzvah of repentance, he categorizes and outlines the respective punishments for a number of theological sins. Among those he labels "heretic," with no claim in the World to Come—"rather, they are cut off and destroyed, and banished due to the greatness of their evil and sin"—are those who concede that there is only one God, but attribute to Him anthropomorphic characteristics (*Mishneh Torah*, Laws of Repentance 3:6–7).

Rabbi Abraham ben David (Ravad) harshly criticized this claim. "Greater men than he [i.e., Maimonides]," Ravad defiantly proclaims, have believed in some form of divine corporeality.

> Why has he called such a person a heretic? There are many people greater than and superior to him who adhere to such a belief on the basis of what they have seen in verses of Scripture and, even more, in the words of those *aggadot* that corrupt right opinion about religious matters.[6]

The Ravad here should not be confused as defending anthropomorphism as theologically valid. His critique should rather be seen as attempting to correct what he sees as a flaw in Maimonides's theological focus. In opposition to Maimonides, Ravad refuses to make the search for truth the exclusive religious focus, much less the singular condition for religious excellence. Believing in corporeality does not make a person a heretic, in his view, because Judaism is not a philosophical religion concerned exclusively, or even primarily, with philosophical truth. Judaism is, rather, a halakhic religion concerned with bringing an awareness of God into everyday life. Halakha, to the contrary, is what makes this goal achievable, not only for elite intellectuals but for a wide range of individuals and communities. Thus Ravad represents a fundamental shift away from the primacy of philosophy, which he rejects as the sole legitimate arbiter of religious status, and toward the ways in which living Jewish communities mediate their relationship with God.[7]

The Ravad, then, saw the halakha as a construction of reality within which one strives to achieve and maintain a sense of God's presence. A pious Jew who understands God through his reading of the Bible is not outside the community. What is most important is how you live, not how you think. In other words, halakha itself, the collective culture of the Jewish people, mediates the encounter with the Divine. In this, the Ravad seems much closer to the spirit of the Talmud than does Maimonides. He found intolerable and religiously misguided—one might say, anti-Jewish—the notion of basing claims of heresy on such abstract philosophical grounds, for this was to him very much a secondary area of religious concern, in no way central to the thrust of the Jewish mission. One is part of Judaism as long as one's spiritual aspirations are pursued within the collective culture of halakha.

I am inclined to agree with Ravad that, in the midst of his philosophical passion, Maimonides at times may have disconnected himself from the living community of Israel. For when we look at what living Judaism is about, it is indeed not a philosophical system. The community gathers around shared rituals, symbols, moments of prayer. It creates a discourse of relational language within the community that is tied to an encompassing awareness of God through halakha. When a son puts on tefillin, he has now entered into a language that he shares with his father, and with all Jews throughout history who put on tefillin. That experience of being part of a religious discourse is itself a form of attunement to God-consciousness.

Judaism is fundamentally the building of a *community* suffused with God-consciousness. Because its communal aspirations are inherent to its identity and inextricable from its end goal, it must present, before anything else, a viable communal way of life. Maimonides holds a different ideal: the single individual who is the intellectual lover, who explores the cosmos to find how God's wisdom is manifested in nature. It is for this reason that Maimonides, in this area, cannot be considered normative but must be marginalized. For all its great benefits, intellectual meditation is not a form of collective life. It does not animate a living community with shared memories and appointed meeting times and places. For the Jewish people throughout the centuries, halakha has been the access point for communal religiosity.

For Maimonides, it becomes necessary to step out of the four cubits of halakha to become a lover of God. A truth searcher, he admits the ultimate difficulty of attaining satisfactory knowledge of God. Still, the quest to understand the true nature of divinity is for him the ultimate religious mode, the sphere of divine love and joy. For halakhic Jews, by contrast, ultimate joy is found not in cosmic contemplation, but in contemplating a beautiful *etrog*, building a beautiful sukkah, lighting beautiful Hanukkah candles. Through the intimate language of the community we express our desire to encounter God and feel God's presence in our life. Religious joy is sought and discovered within the mediative language of the community. Claiming that language, I enter into the religious reality, a reality that is suddenly soaked with religious symbols, religious language, religious forms of life. Claiming that language, I am suddenly enveloped by a system that points everywhere to God. For Maimonides, the imperative to "know" God ("In all your ways, know Him" [Prov. 3:6]) is intellectual. I see it not cognitively, but as the experience of a lover—as Adam, in the "biblical sense," knew Eve. Thus to know God in all your ways is to seek to cultivate the intuitive sense of God's presence in every living human moment. It connects us to historical memory in the way the holidays are observed, to the God of Creation through the laws of the Sabbath. Halakha's great power is to grab us and direct our attention toward the service of God in all situations. It is the striving to embrace all of life under the awareness of God's presence that transforms its practice into the act of a lover. It is experiential intimacy, not intellectual excellence, that halakha both offers and demands.

Communal versus Individual Spirituality

The notion of a communal spirituality is so essential in understanding the theology underpinning halakha that it is worthwhile to take a moment to elaborate upon its basis. One of the deep tensions in Jewish tradition is the role of the individual within a culture in which community is the central organizing spiritual category. According to traditional halakha, certain central prayers require a minyan of ten men, which in the collective Jewish imagination becomes the very symbol of community, the most irreducible unit of religious experience. The source of this communal religious construct is discovered through an interpretation of the verse "That I may be sanctified in the midst of the Israelite people" (Lev. 22:32). The intertwining of sanctification with community lies at the very root-structure of Jewish theology.

It is a salient contrast to many other religious formations, and in particular contemporary formulations of the religious quest, that the spiritual pilgrimage to Judaism does not begin with the "leap of the alone to the alone," to draw upon the German theologian Meister Eckhart's important phrase. Granted, such a significant thinker as Rabbi Soloveitchik, of blessed memory, glorifies the "lonely man" in his writings. For example, he claims that only the lonely individual is creative:

> Why was it necessary to create lonely man?... The originality and creativity of man are rooted in his loneliness experience, not in his social awareness ... Social man is superficial: he imitates, he emulates. Lonely man is profound: he creates, he is original.[8]

Nevertheless, I question the importance assigned to the single individual by traditional Judaism. Fundamentally, Judaism is the way of life of a community and provides understanding for someone who seeks to build a spiritual life within the language and structures of community.

This emphasis is found clearly in its primary holidays. The three pilgrimage festivals of Passover, Shavuot, and Sukkot all center around tying the living community to its historical identity. The holidays of Judaism, unlike Christianity, for example, do not refer to the life of a single individual. As great and revered a prophet as was Moses, we do not celebrate his life-cycle events. Celebration refers to community and takes place within community. To become enchanted by the story of the community, by its historical drama, by the spiritual experience of togetherness—this is what mediates religious vitality in Judaism.

Our history as a community begins in Egypt, where we first transcended our familial identity into that of a broader collective. The
movement from a family story to a communal story begins when
Jacob's children "go down" into Egypt and prosper and grow. The first
vital symbol of identification with community is the fact that we were
slaves to Pharaoh in Egypt. This fact is given ritual primacy as the
father's first instruction to his child. The Passover seder is an attempt
to create a collective memory of the Jew reliving the slavery of his community and the experience of liberation. It is within the ambience of
the memory of slavery that collective identity is forged. Future generations, in order to remain faithful to and unified by this founding communal spirit, must first go through the experience of identification
with a slave people in Egypt.

The other Jewish festivals key into this same sense of collective
identification with other facets of the founding ancestral journey.
After the Exodus follows the encampment at Mount Sinai, the awe-
some, surreal experience of God's presence there, the receiving of the
Ten Commandments—all experienced within the collective matrix.
Man and woman are not alone at Sinai, but among their people.
Similarly, Sukkot, which celebrates the sojourn in the desert that fol-
lowed Sinai, also partakes in the experience of the collective. In
Judaism, then, one begins to find a deeper spiritual reality only
within the community.

For this reason, it is possible to experience great religious joy within
Judaism simply through appreciating the gift given by one's parents of their
connection to Jewish history. While the verse recited by traditional Jews
every morning at prayer—"This is my God and I will enshrine Him; the
God of my father, and I will exalt Him" (Exod. 15:2)—expresses both a
personal and communal mode of divine encounter, my own intuition is
that halakhic Jewish theology strongly favors the latter.

This communal focus puts me in respectful opposition to a number of important modern Jewish theologians. Most notable among
these is Heschel, who evokes so poignantly the pathos of the personal
relationship with God. By contrast, I find the tradition pointing me to
educate both myself and other Jews by cultivating a deep sense of the

"God of my father." Jewish spirituality begins with the gift of history, of living traditions. It is out of that communal experience that we may begin to nurture individual spirituality. Keeping well in mind the Rabbinic teaching, "He who saves one life is as if he saved the whole world (BT *Sanhedrin* 37a)," I nonetheless hold that the modern Israeli philosopher and social critic Yeshayahu Leibowitz saw it clearer than most when he insisted that Judaism is first and foremost an institutional religion shaping the collective life of the Jewish people.

Throughout Jewish history, halakha has served as both this community's shared spiritual language and the normative structure for a way of life that nurtures and enhances the communal spirit. While halakha does not seek to exhaust the range of personal religious experience, it does provide a framework for how to serve God within the covenantal community. In further chapters, I will emphasize the ways in which community is transcended and why there is a need for a spiritual moment outside of halakha, outside the collective, as a source for the self-correction of communal religion. Moreover, individual appropriations, personal meanings, can be found in what I refer to as the second stage in halakhic life. There becomes available a movement of individual religious appropriation. Nevertheless, the individual's pilgrimage as a Jew begins by first identifying with the suffering condition of the children in Egypt and then preparing to move to Sinai and participate in the collective covenantal moment of Judaism. Mitzvah and ritual—the emphasis of halakha—constitute a means of creating a shared language and way of life organized around the shared covenantal commitment and the values it represents.

My personal experience of Jewish meaning both informs and is informed by these intuitions. When I first began to put on tefillin at my bar mitzvah, my father showed me how to set the boxes correctly, how to wrap the leather straps, which verses to recite. I recall vividly knowing, even then, that there was a profound bond, a language we shared: potent symbols that evoked meaning in my father and thus by the calculus of the religious collective became for me the possibility of connecting myself to all of Israel. Many years later, when as an adult I put the covering of the sukkah on our home in Montreal, my son Donniel joined me. At the time a very young man, in his early teens, he looked at me and said, "*Abba*, I'll do this with my children, too." He knew even then that as we covered the sukkah together he was being introduced to a language that reinforced his connection to the chain of Jewish history. Halakhic ritual, then, provides a dramatic way in which to enter into the living history of the Jewish people. As historical reenactments and great period pieces like to claim, "*You are there*": part of the drama of liberation at Egypt, of receiving the Torah at Sinai, of the newly free people moving haltingly but inexorably from the desert to the Promised Land. It is our story, and in telling it and reliving it, we create a Jewish people.

2

TOWARD A GOD-INTOXICATED HALAKHA

God-Consciousness: Halakha as an Educational System

From the previous chapter, it emerges that there are two important ways in which halakha, framed as a communally mediated religious system dedicated to seeking God's presence in every aspect of life, can function as a vital spiritual resource for the Jewish people. For those interested in deepening their involvement with the Jewish community, perhaps seeking meaning in an enhanced identification with their historical family, halakhic experimentation can serve as an entryway to collective spiritual life. For those who accept upon themselves the authority of the halakhic system, thereby embracing more expansive modes of halakhic commitment, this way of life holds out the possibility for ever-deepening meaning derived from the pursuit and evolving experience of God-consciousness. Because these two dimensions of halakha hold the potential to speak to people at different stages in their religious search, it is only appropriate that the halakha itself be framed differently for these different groups.

For those seeking an experiential encounter with the Jewish tradition to gain a sense of the tradition as it is lived, halakha should be engaged as an open-ended educational framework rather than a binding normative one. This approach should not be mistaken for a form of apologetics, as it is based upon an understanding of halakha's essential purpose: the cultivation of individual and communal God-consciousness. (I am grateful to Professor Yehuda Gellman for showing me powerful trends within the Hassidic tradition that seem to speak in this way—in some cases interpreting mitzvot to mean "suggestions" or "counsel" about how most fully to experience the presence of God in one's life.) It is legitimate, I believe, to bracket the question of halakha's putative authority, because authority is by nature a secondary feature of halakhic life. Operating selectively within the halakhic system enables a person to become attuned to the melodies and rhythms of religious experience, to live with certain symbols and reflect upon the ways in which they inspire God-consciousness or detract from it. Halakha enables those at this stage of their religious exploration to experience Judaism in the way it is lived and to reflect upon its resonances within their daily life. As such, it holds out the possibility for a new channel of relationship to God, a new way of experiencing God's presence, mediated through the life of the traditional religious community.

In this context, the practice of halakha operates as a kind of educational experience: learning new ways of participating in community, of acculturating oneself to life with the Jewish family, and of investigating the effects of ritual structures upon one's daily experience and sense of meaning. When I was a congregational rabbi, sometimes people who approached me with a desire to learn would frame their search by asking, "How do Jews Jew?" What, in other words, is the way of life of this community? For example, they seem to congregate on the Sabbath and certain festivals. What is the significance of this collective experience? Is there a role for individual expression within this rigorously disciplined communal way of life? Approaching halakha in this experimental-educational spirit thus fulfills its purpose as a vehicle for enhanced God-consciousness within a framework of enhanced participation in the Jewish community; concrete, living understanding of the

Jewish community; and emotional identification with the Jewish community. It provides an opportunity to know something of this way of life from within, the aspects of communal religious experience that are intangible: the "flavor" or "taste," the kind of understanding that is impossible to absorb through books, conversation, or any other secondary source.

It is extremely important that we create a space within our theology, and within our communities, for the legitimate (though not exclusive) positive understanding of halakha as a selective educational system, and not only as a legal system. For modern Jews who seek access to the lived experience of Jewish community, it is not merely a "tactical" mistake to present halakha in terms of principles of authority, obligations, and the sinful consequences of failure to uphold all of the mitzvot. It is a failure of the religious imagination and ultimately a failure of the Jewish community. The legalistic weight of halakha should be lifted completely and without theological compunction. Legalism and authoritarianism are not the best ways to educate a person to begin a way of life, and the overemphasis upon absolute authority claims and legalistic minutiae so prevalent among many Orthodox Jews today belies halakha's essence and does a grave disservice to the profound potential it holds for today's diverse Jewish population. Halakha, derived from the Hebrew root that means "walking," should be framed as a religious path, a process of ever-evolving spiritual sensitivity. Though traditionally halakha has predominantly been represented as a legal-normative system requiring total commitment, we need not necessarily relate to it that way.

To be clear, asserting that halakha can be framed legitimately as an educational system is not necessarily synonymous with giving up on it as a disciplined system of authoritative laws. Halakha can function differently for different types of individuals and communities, meeting people at varying stages of their spiritual interest, experience, passion, and commitment. It can serve for some as an open-ended journey among various possibilities for enhanced God-consciousness—one mode of living with the tradition—and for others, who desire to integrate it into their lives in a more encompassing fashion, as a system of normative obligation that offers ever-expanding potentials for God-intoxication. For those who choose to make this shift to a normative relationship to halakha (or are born into it and choose to remain), a new and weighty set of questions is likely to emerge around the central issue with which I opened this book: What happens when halakhic commitment conflicts with moral conscience? Does an individual allow the authority of the system to override personal moral integrity, to define morality by fiat? What other theological options are available for negotiating this type of dilemma?

God-Intoxication: Halakha as a Normative System

I have explained the significance of halakha with an emphasis on its function and goal of enriching God-consciousness. Admittedly, this is not a dimension of halakha that is often emphasized or even mentioned by those most rigorously involved in its study and/or observance. Most commonly, halakha is framed as a system of duties and prohibitions. Granted, God is seen as the source of obligation, but far more rarely as an active, accessible presence within the patterns and rhythms of its daily performance. This more detached conception of God within halakha is deeply embedded in the ethos of the halakhic world and often seems to be at cross-purposes with cultivating a sense of ongoing spiritual search—as a way not of encouraging but rather avoiding the personal religious quest.

One of the most important terms in the halakhic lexicon describes a person's status upon performing an obligatory act. Upon doing so, a person has *yatza yeday chovatah*: fulfilled—literally "exited from"—his or her duty. One effect of this reassuring and oft-repeated declaration is to affirm that, in performing a particular set of halakhic requirements, we have done what is required of us. Halakhic practice thus comes to be seen as an end in itself, the fulfillment of a finite set of duties, without being contextualized within a deepening of the relationship with God.

This mind-set would not seem likely to nurture the kind of religious personality who strives for ever-increasing awareness of the divine presence, perennially concerned with bridging a nagging sense of personal distance from God. When the relational feature of God-consciousness is present, how can a person ever truly feel that he or she has fulfilled his or her duty? When the currency animating the relationship is love, how can one ever have done enough? This seems to be the kind of halakhic personality toward which Maimonides urges his readers to aspire in the evocative final chapter to his "Laws of Repentance." After describing, in negative terms, the religious personality who serves God out of fear, he proceeds to present the positive ideal:

> It is the level of Abraham our Forefather, whom God called, "My lover," because he worshipped only out of love. And it is the level that God commanded us through Moses, as it says: "And you must love the Lord your God" (Deut. 6:5). And in the moment that a person will love God with the appropriate love—immediately he will perform all the mitzvot out of love.
>
> … And what is the appropriate love? Thus: That a person should love God with a great, powerful, overwhelming love, until his soul is connected to the love of God and he finds himself ruminating upon it always, as if he is sick with lovesickness, such that his mind is never free from the love of that woman and he ruminates on her always, whether sitting or standing, eating or drinking. Even more than that should the love of God be in the hearts of God's lovers, ruminating upon God always, as God commanded us: [And you must love your God] with all your heart, and with all your soul (Deut. 6:5). And this is what Solomon said by way of metaphor: "For I am lovesick" (Song of Songs 2:5). And all of Song of Songs is a metaphor for this.[1]

In the broad cultural sweep of individuals and communities who identify themselves as halakhically committed, this lifestyle has often not succeeded in cultivating this type of personality. For halakha to fulfill its potential and purpose, I would suggest, halakhic communities must retool their relationship to the system in the spirit here articulated by Maimonides. Rather than encouraging a sense of satisfaction in their service of God through halakhic practice, we must advance an ethos of worship that is open-ended and experiential, that creates a powerful attraction based in part on a powerful sense that our sensitivity to God's presence can always be enhanced. Embracing halakha as an encompassing system of normative obligation, touching ever more diverse facets of daily life, should *amplify* this quest—and not, as is often the case, help to mute it.

Admittedly, this has not always been my own halakhic lens. As a rabbi for eighteen years and a teacher for forty, I rarely placed God-intoxication at the forefront of halakhic education or practice. I tried to show how halakha works to bring its practitioners into a deeper sense of family identity, and the types of significance its symbolic system might inspire. But I cannot say that, as a rabbi, I attempted to educate my community to become God-intoxicated (*holat-ahava*, lit. "lovesick"). The only form of intoxication I can recall clearly from this time derived not from halakha but from the scotch that was brought out at the *Kiddush* after Saturday morning services.

Moreover, I have long been aware of modern philosophical approaches to halakha that oppose linking it to an experiential aware-ness of God. The important Israeli philosopher Yeshayahu Leibowitz argues that there can be no understanding or awareness of God beyond executing God's revealed will as expressed in the commandments. For Leibowitz, the notion of being in the presence of God is identical to and exhausted by the practice of halakha. There is no sense of God-consciousness independent of halakhic ritual. Understood in this way, halakha can hardly be linked to a religious ethos of God-intoxication. Halakha itself is both the exclusive expression of belief and the sum total of religious experience.

Given that most existing halakhic communities do not seem imbued with a God-focused halakhic sensibility, and given philosoph-ical stances like Leibowitz's that characterize such a focus as, in any event, out of sync with halakha's true religious nature, it is reasonable to ask why I find this dimension of halakha so important to emphasize. I have shown above how it can provide a theological basis for legitimating the view of halakha as an open-ended educational system. But that is only part of the story. Why is it important that God-consciousness figure so prominently in the characterization of halakha, when for so many it functions as a way of neutralizing this type of spiritual search?

God-Intoxication and Halakhic Self-Correction

My answer is that I believe viewing halakha through this lens can better equip us to negotiate conflicts between the requirements of the system and the demands of moral conscience. A God-focused approach to halakha can provide not only an enriched sense of spiritual community, but also an interpretive strategy with the potential to impact the evolution of halakhic practice on both the personal and communal levels. Bringing God-consciousness into halakhic discourse confronts each individual with the question, which God? Who is the God I strive to serve through halakha? Or perhaps more precisely: given that Jewish tradition, beginning with the Bible itself, presents many different images of God, which of these images do we have in mind, to bring more fully into our spiritual awareness, when observing halakha?

Taken seriously as a question embedded in the heart of the halakhic project, our answer or answers will naturally impact heavily upon the quality and development of halakhic life. If we accept the premise that halakha is not in its essence about promoting a set of values or building a certain type of community through collective forms of life, but about the driving purpose of these values and forms—that is, to cultivate a certain quality of relationship with God—we must begin with Buber's observation that "the imageless God has many images."[2] Warrior, father, lover, king, spouse—which of these images animates halakhic commitment and colors halakhic experience? If the purpose of the practice is to structure a relationship with God, this would seem to be a question of determinative importance. A person struck by God's awesome power as a warrior and general will have a very different relationship to halakhic life than one who feels shielded by God's grace as a protector of the weak and downtrodden. Since halakha structures the spiritual environments of the people who live within it, these two people, nurtured by very different sensibilities of halakhic meaning, will develop in different ways. Naturally, the halakha they practice will develop with them along the same lines—even though externally, their practices may seem similar or identical.

The critical significance of this question should now be clear. Indeed, I would argue that it is essentially this question Moses poses to God directly at one of the central moments of his life, a moment of great spiritual intimacy following the dramatic climax of his advocacy for the lives of the Jewish people and the continuation of the Jewish story following the sin of the Golden Calf:

> "Now, if I have truly gained Your favor, pray let me know Your ways, that I may know You and continue in Your favor. Consider, too, that this nation is Your people." And He said, "I will go in the lead and will lighten your burden." And he said to Him, "Unless You go in the lead, do not make us leave this place. For how shall it be known that Your people have gained Your favor unless You go with us, so that we may be distinguished, Your people and I, from every people on the face of the earth?"
>
> And the Lord said to Moses, "I will also do this thing that you have asked; for you have truly gained My favor and I have singled you out by name." He said, "Oh, let me behold Your Presence!" And He answered, "I will make all My goodness pass before you, and I will proclaim before you the name Lord, and the grace that I grant and the compassion that I show. But," He said, "you cannot see My face, for man may not see Me and live." And the Lord said, "See, there is a place near Me. Station yourself on the rock and, as My Presence passes by, I will put you in a cleft of the rock and shield you with My hand until I have passed by. Then I will take My hand away and you will see My back; but My face must not be seen."
>
> (Exod. 33:13–23)

Moses formulates his plea for divine knowledge in relational, not ontological, terms. He seeks, in short, to deepen his relationship with God. God's response, the revelation of what are known as the "Thirteen Attributes," seems pitched to address precisely this need:

> The Lord came down in a cloud; He stood with him there, and proclaimed the name Lord. The Lord passed before him and proclaimed: "The Lord! the Lord! a God compassionate and gracious, slow to anger, abounding in kindness and faithfulness, extending kindness to the thousandth generation, forgiving iniquity, transgression, and sin...."
>
> (EXOD. 34:5–7)

The Talmud understands God's response in the same relational spirit, midrashically contextualizing this revelation as the outcome of a longer conversation between Moses and God. In their narrative, following the Golden Calf incident, Moses has fallen into deep despair over the possibility of the Jewish people's spiritual recovery. In response, God offers the Thirteen Attributes, with the explanation, "Whenever Israel sins, let them recite this in its proper order and I will forgive them" (BT *Rosh Hashana* 17b). The attributes of a forgiving, loving God provide a guiding framework for the evolving character of the spiritual systems in which we live.

Maimonides makes this point even more sharply in the *Guide for the Perplexed*. According to Maimonides, it is impossible to know God at all. What we can know is that there are moral attributes that mediate a relationship with God. I may have a deep personal intuition that there is an Other; but how is my intuition nurtured? It is nurtured by participating in the ritual life of the community, which enhances the sense of a presence, a reality, giving shape and direction to inchoate spiritual longings. We cannot know God, but we can know how to live with God. We can know, for example, that God requires decency, compassion, and justice. For Maimonides, the lived experience of that imagery constitutes my understanding of God. I always relate to halakha with that question. Does halakha, which structures lived experience, bring me into ever-deepening contact with a God that wants me to act justly?

The answer to the two requests that He, may He be exalted, gave him consisted in His promising him to let him know all His attributes, making it known to him that they are His actions, and teaching him that His essence cannot be grasped as it really is. Yet He drew his attention to a subject of speculation through which he can apprehend to the furthest extent that is possible for man.... For his saying, "Show me Thy ways, that I may know Thee," indicates that God, may He be exalted, is known through His attributive qualifications; for when he would know the "ways," he would know Him.... The proof of the assertion that the thing, the apprehension of which was promised to him, was the actions of God, may He be exalted, is the fact that what was made known to him were simply pure attributes of action: "merciful and gracious, long-suffering." It is then clear that the "ways"—for a knowledge of which he had asked and which, in consequence, were made known to him—are the actions proceeding from God, may He be exalted.[3]

We find the template of the Thirteen Attributes appropriated by Jeremiah in a climactic exhortation that concisely articulates the goal of spiritual worship:

Thus said the Lord: Let not the wise man glory in his wisdom; Let not the strong man glory in his strength; Let not the rich man glory in his riches. But *only in this should one glory: In his earnest devotion to Me. For I the Lord act with kindness, Justice, and equity in the world; For in these I delight—declares the Lord.*

(JER. 9:22–23; EMPHASIS ADDED)

This prophetic verse is tied explicitly by Maimonides to its antecedent in the Thirteen Attributes and further interpreted by him into a capsule description of the ideal Jewish "way of life":

For when explaining in this verse the noblest ends, [Jeremiah] does not limit them only to the apprehension of Him, may He be exalted. For if this were his purpose, he would have said: "But let him that glory, glory in this, that he understand, and know Me—" and have stopped there; or he would have said: "that he understand and know Me that I am One"; or he would have said: "that I have no figure," or "that there is none like Me," or something similar. But he says that one should glory in the apprehension of Myself and in the knowledge of My attributes, by which he means His actions, as we have made clear with reference to its dictum: "Show me Thy ways...." In this verse, he makes it clear to us that those actions that ought to be known and imitated are "loving-kindness, judgment, and righteousness." ... Then he completes the notion by saying: "For in these things I delight, says the Lord." He means that it is My purpose that there should come from you "loving-kindness, righteousness, and judgment in the earth" in the way we have explained with regard to the Thirteen Attributes: namely, that the purpose should be assimilation to them and that this should be our way of life."[4]

In a halakhic way of life infused by this spirit, a perspective focused on God-consciousness can act as a guiding framework for the evolution of halakha, functioning as an important corrective to the types of halakhic decision making (and decision avoidance) that tend to trigger moral conflict among many modern Jews. To continually ask the question, *Which God are we worshipping?* is to introduce a critical catalyst for self-correction. It is to offer a way for individuals and communities to negotiate aspects of the tradition they find problematic, allowing personal subjectivity as a way of both deepening and critically evaluating one's religious practice. Rather than searching for moral guidance within the legal precedents and exegetical maneuvering of the halakhic library, as has sadly become the common default for a wide variety of halakhic Jews, we must search for it in the image of God our moral conscience desires to learn from and compels us to choose. When God told Abraham about his plot to destroy the people of Sodom, Abraham's response was not to run to the library and crack open a book. There is a natural impulse about what is decent and just. We should allow that impulse to surface within our religious system, rather than burying or dismissing it. In this way, a God-intoxicated halakha fully emancipates the natural religious yearning that may feel nurtured by the halakhic system, yet suppressed and constricted by the moral conflicts that arise within it.

Thus, God-consciousness is not only a theological principle of halakha, but a hermeneutic one. Before proceeding to work through any halakhic issue that may come up, there must be an understanding of the image of God that will be guiding me in my analysis.

Who Defines What Is Moral?

An obvious and oft-asked question arises: doesn't the halakhic system claim ultimate moral authority under its own, self-legitimating jurisdiction? Thus, in instances when personal moral intuition conflicts with tradition, from a religious perspective would not the prudent and/or prescribed path be to question the intuition and defer to tradition, instead of the other way around? Even if we hold that moral inclination is deeply connected to the worship of God, we must acknowledge—as I emphasized positively above—that its origin is an impulse that resides deep within personal subjectivity. Is it religiously incumbent that we allow tradition to override subjectivity and define what constitutes morality for each individual? Or is there room for more of a conversation between traditional norms and moral intuition that emerges naturally through the course of living? Can religion challenge us to abandon basic moral convictions? For example, most decent people of good faith know that beating a helpless child is wrong. Having someone suffer because of the crimes of someone else is wrong. To judge someone with discrimination or otherwise without justification is wrong. If someone is lying on the floor bleeding, the right thing is to call an ambulance. We don't need Kantian ethics to know it is necessary for us to respond to the needs of the sick and have compassion for the elderly. We also don't need, it seems, the imperatives of Scripture. And

yet should we allow religious authority to override other moral judg-
ments drawn from the same subjective source? Is there room for this
independent moral thinking within the halakhic system?

I have been asked this question often and in different forms.
Sometimes the challenge is emotional and ad hominem, but it also
comes in more substantive and compelling forms. Interestingly, it is
rarely posed as an abstract appeal to divine authority. As I argued in my
book *A Living Covenant*, the nature of the Jewish people's relationship
with God as portrayed by the Bible and enlarged by the Talmudic Sages
not only legitimates finite individual perspectives but celebrates them
as constitutive of the covenantal religious imperative. Morality is, of
course, one of the most central facets of any individual's value system.
Nevertheless, even for those who might validate moral intuition generally as a factor in halakhic decision making, we immediately run into
the question, who defines what is moral?

The ad hominem argument reads something like this: As a living,
lived tradition, halakha can claim great sages, saints, and devoted
laypeople throughout a great variety of historical and geographical set-
tings. Pious men and women of unassailable character have lived their
entire lives passionately committed to the halakhic system, without
necessarily feeling or expressing the types of moral conflicts I
described in the Introduction. Given this history of ancestral loyalty to
the totality of halakha, how can we be certain that our own ethical
intuitions have not been corrupted by influences alien to the spirit of
halakha? Can we trust modern liberal sensibilities, for example, to be
the ground of our morality in relationship to a two-thousand-year-old
tradition? Isn't the halakha inherently moral because of its living religious claims, the individuals and communities who have adhered to it
over the centuries, lived and died in order for it to be passed down in
its current form? The luminaries of previous generations did not seem
to question its morality.

The rhetoric used to challenge the validity of personal morality is
thus often framed as an insult to the ethical sensibilities of our predecessors. Often cited in this context are people like Rabbi Yisrael Ha-
Kohen Kagan, known as the Hafetz Hayim, a twentieth-century

halakhist with a widespread reputation for saintliness. Thus the challenge has been put to me in this way on more than one occasion: *Do you think you're more ethical than the Hafetz Hayim?*

Within this ad hominem criticism is embedded, however, a more substantive critique that deserves to be addressed. In short: How can I give weight to my moral critique of halakha if the moral claim is not self-evident—if other moral possibilities are available? How can I allow my liberal twenty-first-century way of life to guide me in interpreting the halakha when, in fact, other moral perspectives are available from different traditions? Even if we agree with Maimonides that "demonstrative truth" can serve as a basis for reinterpreting the whole Bible,[5] morality does not seem to belong to this definitive philosophical category (the provenance, for example, of the demonstrable eternality of the universe).

Given this acknowledgment, doesn't the possibility of other moral interpretations cancel out the possibility of certainty in my own moral convictions? Shouldn't I weaken my reliance on my own morality when other viable "moralities" are available? Why should I allow my (admittedly!) contingent, highly situated moral perspectives to override the eternal weight of Torah law? Is this anything short of chutzpah?

The natural extension of this line of reasoning is to totally neutralize, and perhaps in some instances pathologize, any personal moral claims that might come into conflict with traditional sensibilities or demands. This kind of criticism seems aimed to cultivate a sense of moral self-doubt, to cast a permanent shadow on the certainty of my moral conviction. Once effectively contained, the prospect of reinterpreting long-standing traditions based upon such claims becomes nonsensical. This perspective thus clearly undermines personal morality both as a theological value and as a hermeneutic principle.

It seems reasonable to ask what effect the neutralization/invalidation of personal conscience might have upon the development of the religious personality, both individually and communally. If I begin to second-guess my moral convictions, I am essentially placing a religious priority self-negation. I am using sacrificial imagery—not the Abraham who argues at Sodom, but the Abraham who mutely prepares his son for slaughter at Moriah—as my model for religious emulation, abnegating a critical element of my identity in the service of God. What kind of human being then stands in the service of God? A person, it stands to reason, who is drained of moral passion, having forcibly suppressed that part of him- or herself. Morality has become external, a matter of following rules rather than becoming attuned to an internal voice. We need not make the claim that personal morality constitutes ultimate truth in order to encourage its robust cultivation as a spiritual value. The fact that certain voices and sensibilities speak to and compel us, that we choose to live by them—this is enough. To deny that voice is to deny our human identity.

I do not believe that the tradition itself demands this kind of sacrifice or portrays the sacrificial model as the only valid religious orientation. There is another option, another strain found within Rabbinic thinking that legitimates this type of questioning based on the reliance upon a personal moral voice. A prominent instance can be found within a midrashic discussion about the *mamzer*, the child conceived through proscribed sexual relations. The discussion begins with an interpretation of a verse in Ecclesiastes that refers obliquely to the "tears of the oppressed":

> "I further observed all the oppression that goes on under the sun: the tears of the oppressed, with none to comfort them; and the power of their oppressors—with none to comfort them" (Eccles. 4:1). Daniel the tailor interpreted this verse as pertaining to *mamzerim*. "The tears of the oppressed": their mothers transgressed, and these poor ones are excluded; this one's father committed incest, but what has he done and why should he be affected. [There is] "none to comfort him," [but rather they are subjected to] "the power of their oppressors": this refers to Israel's Great Sanhedrin, who come at them with Torah's power and exclude them, applying [the verse,] "No *mamzer* shall be admitted into the congregation of the Lord" (Deut. 23:3). "None to comfort them"—the Holy One says, "It is for me to comfort them." Yes, in this world some are spurned, but as for the future, Zechariah has said, "I see a people all of gold" (Zech. 4:2).
>
> (*Midrash Rabbah*, Leviticus 32:8)

In Daniel the tailor, the midrash presents a character lodging a sharp moral critique not only at a deeply rooted biblical statute but equally the Rabbinic power elite who enforce it. Why, one might ask, should they be considered at fault for implementing Torah law? At the heart of Daniel's indictment of the Sanhedrin seems to be their failure to reinterpret the verses pertaining to *mamzer* based on a moral aversion to both its nature and its consequences: the extreme social isolation of children based upon their parents' crimes. According to the midrash, God Himself endorses Daniel's stinging critique of the moral apathy of the Rabbinic leadership, thus presenting a complex theological picture in which God is bound by the human interpretations of Torah law— even though God knows the law is immoral.

Here the midrash places God in sympathy with the sense of human impotence religious people may feel when confronted by (perhaps otherwise brilliant) religious leaders who seem to deactivate their moral conscience in deference to the "plain meaning" of biblical verses—the halakhic status quo. What may seem at first blush like piety, this midrash suggests, is actually the opposite, a form of behavior despised by God. To live by halakha, in this instance, is to perpetuate immorality and oppression. To emulate God is to allow particular moral perspectives to surface and in turn allow those perspectives to critique and correct the tradition in places where its ethical sensibility has perhaps come to lag behind the tradition's core values, ideals, and end goals (which, it bears repeating, the midrash identifies with God, the God Daniel insists upon worshipping). The affirmation of halakhic immorality and bold identification of its source at the highest levels of Jewish spiritual leadership thus create an opening to a moral critique of the tradition.

Other perspectives within the Jewish tradition have viewed the issue of *mamzer* very differently. The moral critique presented above, while seemingly endorsed by the editor of an authoritative collection of midrash, has proved far from universally self-evident. A Talmudic legal discussion about the number of generations included within the *mamzer* ban turns to a reflection upon the reasoning behind it. Two prominent rabbis express the position that such a discussion is irrelevant, taking it as fact that God will bring about the death of *mamzerim*, obviating the marriage issue. The Talmudic editor points out that this position seems in contradiction with an earlier Rabbinic decree: "*Mamzers* … are prohibited [i.e., from marrying Jews], and their prohibition is perpetual." Why go to the trouble of legislating an impossibility?

> Rabbi Zeira said: It was explained to me by Rav Yehuda: a [publicly] known *mamzer* lives; an unknown *mamzer* does not live. A *mamzer* that is partially known lives until three generations; more than that, he does not live.
>
> (BT *Yevamot* 78b)

According to these rabbis, the marriage prohibition against those bearing *mamzer* status serves an important communal purpose, protecting non-*mamzers* from the possibility of unknowingly marrying one and thus becoming tainted by what seemed to be considered a kind of spiritual disease. Rashi's commentary articulates concisely what seems implicit in the Talmud's words, which he begins by quoting: "'Mamzers *do not live*': So that they will not be able to infect the non-*mamzers* of their generations." So important is the protection extended by the Torah's *mamzer* statute that when it fails to achieve its purpose of protecting Jews (as in the case of undetected *mamzers*), God intervenes with a direct form of damage control. Needless to say, these Talmudic rabbis do not see the social exclusion of *mamzers* as morally problematic, much less as requiring reinterpretation. Moreover, they rely on God to solve the problem and clearly seem to be worshipping a different image of God than does the midrashic Daniel portrayed above. Again we find moral sensitivity bound up intimately with this foundational theological question. The depth of their belief in this benevolent understanding of *mamzer* law is brought home in a startling narrative postscript to the interpretive dispute:

> There was such a person [i.e., an unknown *mamzer*] in the neighborhood of Rabbi Ami. [Rabbi Ami] announced publicly that he was a *mamzer*. [The man thus exposed] wept and wept. [Rabbi Ami] said to him, "I have given you life!" [i.e., because unknown *mamzers* do not live to marry].
>
> (*Leviticus Rabbah* 32)

This orientation toward *mamzer* law is found echoed stridently by the late thirteenth-century commentator Pinchas Halevi of Barcelona. Halevi, like some of his Rabbinic predecessors, looks into *mamzer* law and finds only God's protective beneficence:

> At the root of the precept lies the reason that the engendering of a bastard is very evil, occurring in uncleanness, abominable thought, and sinful counsel. And there is no doubt that the nature of the father is hidden (latent) in the son. Therefore, in His kindness, the Eternal Lord removed the progeny of holiness from him, even as He separated us from every evil thing.[6]

This perspective confronts us dramatically with the substantive question of to what extent subjective moral intuition can be given weight, given that it lacks the proof of a necessary absolute claim. Other moral traditions exist, other valid possibilities and interpretations. How can I privilege my own to the extent of reinterpreting the tradition?

My intent here is not to privilege one strain of Rabbinic thinking over another, though it may be clear where my own intuitions lie. My intent is merely to provide an example of one instance in which particular moral perspectives are given weight, a ground for questioning halakha, even though it does not claim the kind of necessity required by Maimonides to reinterpret the tradition. Neither Halevi nor his Talmudic predecessors cancel out the midrashic interpretation of Daniel, or vice versa. One sees unjust suffering; another sees God's providential protection and love. The point is that even though there existed an alternate interpretation providing a moral justification for *mamzer* law—and so the moral critique cannot be seen to be self-evident, but the product of a particular moral perspective—the intuition of the dissenting, critical voice has validity and halakhic weight as a legitimate spiritual stance within the tradition.

Another instance of a group of sages grappling with divergent moral sensibilities can be found in the Talmudic discussion of the "rebellious son." The Bible presents the case of "a wayward and defiant son, who does not heed his father or mother and does not obey them even after they discipline him" (Deut. 21:18). The punishment for this type of defiance—and its associated behaviors, gluttony and drunkenness—is severe: public stoning. The Talmud grapples explicitly with the moral issue of this disproportionate penalty:

> It has been taught: Rabbi Jose the Galilean said: Did the Torah decree that the rebellious son shall be brought before a court and stoned merely because he ate a *tartemar* [weight measure] of meat and a *log* [liquid measure] of wine?
>
> (BT SANHEDRIN 72A)

In discussing this issue, different rabbis take different stances. One creates such prohibitive procedural requirements for conviction as to essentially render the law nonfunctional. This position seems to reflect a moral problem with the law and attempts to rectify it through internal, exegetical means, rather than open critique or reinterpretation. Another justifies it, claiming that such a person will inevitably come to a bad end, harming others in the process. This perspective sees God's benevolence and protection from the suffering he will invariably cause others. A third approach claims that no such case ever came up or ever was prosecuted—"it never happened and never will happen"—explaining that it is only included in the Torah "that you may study it and receive reward."

These different approaches clearly reflect very different ethical sensibilities—and again, different images of God. The second approach finds no moral fault with the "rebellious son" law. The first and third express a sense of conflict between the law and moral claims but attempt to respond to the problem internally, through halakhic and theological means. If the discussion ended here, we might be left with the impression that internal religious mechanisms provide sufficient means to address potential conflicts between morality and halakha. But it doesn't, instead adding what I understand to be a somewhat ominous, and certainly cautionary, postscript:

> Rabbi Yonatan said: I saw a "stubborn and rebellious son," and
> I sat on his grave.
>
> (BT *SANHEDRIN* 72A)

This final opinion seems to me a fairly searing critique of the moral
hesitation found in the approaches that seek to resolve conflicts of
morality quietly and internally. Perhaps, Rabbi Yonatan seems to say,
these approaches "work" in the world of halakhic methodology or theological speculation. But we should not be smug in our appraisals of
what we actually accomplish through these limited means. In the
world of real lives, and real graves, we must seek bolder solutions.

3

FEMINISM AND APOLOGETICS
Lying in the Presence of God

One of the most glaring moral challenges to halakhic credibility is the situation of the *aguna*—the woman who, by virtue of her husband's recalcitrance or disappearance, is unable to procure his signed consent to a divorce. According to halakha, this woman has no recourse. Unable to remarry, she is relegated to languish in an open-ended legal limbo, emotionally alone—and invariably distressed, given the circumstances that tend to surround such scenarios—yet still considered, in halakhic terminology, the "wife of a husband," a status whose transgression constitutes one of Jewish tradition's severest taboos.

In recent years, there has been a sharp upsurge in interest and activism within the halakhic community toward reforming this morally problematic piece of Jewish law. The public spotlight shone on this issue has provoked a backlash among some powerful halakhic traditionalists. But there are many across the halakhic spectrum who have acknowledged this as a moral issue and sought different methods of addressing it. In a general sense, they can be seen as offering versions of the approaches espoused by the different sages quoted at the end of chapter 2 in response to the morally problematic law of the "rebellious son." Like the Rabbis who create such prohibitive procedural requirements as to essentially render the law nonfunctional, intricate attempts to find creative loopholes within the halakhic system that would release these "bound women" from their state of imprisonment have been offered by modern rabbis of great learning, courage, and sensitivity. Some have been ignored, others maligned; as yet no resolution has been deemed acceptable by a consensus of traditionalist authorities. For those women currently trapped within the traditional divorce procedures, there is no means by which they may become seen, in the eyes of their communities, as legitimately released from their married status. However, notwithstanding the inefficacy of these attempts, they do reflect a moral problem with the law and attempt to rectify it through internal, exegetical means. In the meantime, an optional prenuptial agreement has been formulated for couples entering marriage, in which the husband agrees to give consent in the event that the wife requests a divorce, or face severe financial penalties.

Another response to the *aguna* issue has been internal regulation within halakhic communities. In response to specific situations, ad hoc committees may deploy social pressures and at times violence to compel recalcitrant husbands to give the necessary consent. While appropriate in spirit, this pragmatic approach obviously cannot be relied upon. Some husbands, for whatever reasons, may simply take the punishments meted out while maintaining their recalcitrant stance. This approach also cannot be applied, for obvious reasons, to cases in which the husband has simply disappeared.

Other rabbis, apparently attempting to convey solidarity with the plight of *agunot*, abdicate their moral and halakhic responsibility by describing the issue in terms of an unbearable and inscrutable theological test—for themselves, as rabbis. "This is my personal *akeida* [Abraham's Binding of Isaac]," one major modern Orthodox halakhic authority once told me, referring to his sense of helplessness at not being able to formulate an acceptable halakhic solution based upon available precedents. "*Your akeida?*" I responded. "Is that supposed to bring comfort to the abandoned woman whose life is passing her by?"

This theological posturing, with its distasteful rhetoric of rabbinic helplessness and suffering, nevertheless constitutes an acknowledgment of the moral issue. In a sense, this can be seen as the most openly critical stance that has been offered by traditional rabbis. If my rabbinic colleague had not felt the moral weight of the issue upon him—had he not felt implicated in its shame—there would have been no need to construct such a bombastic, self-aggrandizing response.

I have heard this sentiment echoed by other halakhic authorities as a response to the *aguna* problem. Like Rabbi Simeon above, whose faith in the tradition's ultimate morality in the face of a clearly immoral law led him to claim that there never had been, and never will be, a real-life instance of the rebellious son, these modern-day halakhists seem to seek theological refuge in divine inscrutability. In the same voice that they implicitly criticize the *aguna* law as unfair—invoking the intuitive unfairness of God asking Abraham to sacrifice His beloved son Isaac—they abnegate their responsibility to respond to this moral transgression by invoking Abraham's mute obedience to the unfathomable divine command.

It is important to point out here that these rabbis' position toward halakha is clearly informed by a particular image of God and, moreover, that it is an image of God they have chosen to appropriate from among a broad field. Moreover, it is an image of juristic passivity, one might even say paralysis, that makes for an uncomfortable fit with an endeavor, halakha, whose signature quality over millennia has been the bold, creative intellectual independence of its greatest practitioners.

"I saw a 'stubborn and rebellious son,' and I sat on his grave." And what of the final, nagging voice of Rabbi Yonatan? What of the boy buried six feet in the ground? Not surprisingly, perhaps, this is the voice in the tradition with which I most closely identify. The various internal religious mechanisms applied to the *aguna* problem have failed. Many women still suffer this unjust fate at the tradition's hands. Rabbi Yonatan's caution has gone unheeded by the halakhic authorities of our time. In what I understand to be the spirit of his remark, I find it necessary to offer a more systemic critique of the trends within halakha that have exposed women to such great suffering and risk. I will examine some of the dominant modern Orthodox responses to the moral challenge of feminism and contrast them with the actual treatment of women by halakha. I will expose and reflect upon the images of God that seem to inform the ways women's roles have been constructed by halakhic norms, and I will suggest an alternative approach modeled on a hermeneutic of God-consciousness.

Taken in context, the *aguna* issue is only one painful flashpoint in what has been modernity's most serious and radical moral challenge to traditional Judaism: the emergence of the feminist critique of conventional understandings of gender identity. In order to rigorously examine some modern Orthodox responses to the feminist moral critique of halakha, we should first understand where the main challenges to tradition lie. For the sake of analysis, they can usefully be broken down into three broad spheres of women's experience:

1. *Family life*—that is, women's status within the family system. Is she a dependent, or can she act independently? What kind of room does she have to navigate her own life within the context of marriage?

2. *Ritual life*—in particular, the liturgical experience of the community as it celebrates Jewish religious life within the context of the synagogue. To what extent can a woman be seen as a legitimate and independent religious personality participating in communal worship? Can she be called to the Torah; can she serve as a leader of prayer; can she be included in the quorum of ten?

3. *The public life of the community*—including social and political responsibility—that is, her role in social politics. How public can she be? Do we lose something important and sacred if women are involved in the tumult of political life? Does it undermine the sanctity of the family?

I will take each of these in turn.

Women and Family Life

The Metaphysics of Marriage: Rabbi Joseph B. Soloveitchik

While remaining entrenched on the *aguna* issue and holding fast its resistance to other gender-related concerns carrying a whiff of feminism,[1] modern Orthodoxy has acknowledged the systemic moral challenge of feminism in several ways. Perhaps the most prevalent is a proliferation of apologetic literature by leading Orthodox theologians. The apologetic posture tacitly acknowledges the legitimacy of certain modern, Western values with respect to male-female relationships in its claim that the halakhic tradition actually gives voice to some of these values in powerful and novel ways. No significant traditional halakhic thinker has treated the subject of marriage and family more comprehensively than Rabbi Joseph B. Soloveitchik, whose thoughts on the matter are collected in a book-length volume titled *Family Redeemed*. Drawing upon a variety of Western philosophical traditions—classical ethical philosophy, Kantian metaphysics, existentialist pathos, and a passionate Romantic idealism, for example—he weaves these together with biblical verses and halakhic insights to construct a picture of the Jewish perspective on marriage.

"Marriage," Soloveitchik explains, "is not just a successful partnership, but an existential community."[2] He amplifies the biblical God's assessment that "it is not good for man to be alone" (Gen. 2:18) into an "ontological postulate"—man needs help not only pragmatically but, more to the point, "man needs help ontologically. Another homo-persona is necessary to complete man's existence, to endow it with existential meaning and directedness."[3] The individual human suddenly confronted with spiritual awareness, the "metaphysical man," becomes "burdened with a new awareness, one of inadequacy, illegitimacy, and rootlessness; he was troubled by a great anxiety, by a sickness unto death—fright. In a word, he found himself lonely and forsaken."[4] The purpose of the marital relationship is to redeem man from the spiritual loneliness resulting from his unique status as a "homo absconditus, a 'hidden man' whom no one knows."[5] This unique human quality "expresses itself in the *mysterium magnum* which no one but God can penetrate."[6] It is for this reason—the same reason Eve was created—that man and woman join together. "In order to escape loneliness, man-*absconditus* had to meet woman-mystery."[7]

Soloveitchik presents an essentialist understanding of the spiritual-existential qualities man and woman respectively bring to the relationship. However, he does not judge, or claim that the tradition judges, one to be more valuable than the other. Rather, in his presentation, the differences complement one another, joining to form a whole.

> They have a lot in common…. However, they are also different; their existential experiences are incommensurate. The I-awareness of Adam is totally incomprehensible to Eve, and vice versa. Each of them has a secret which neither will never betray. Man-*persona* and woman-*persona* resemble each other and at the same time do not understand each other. She is *ezer ke-negdo*, his helper and opponent at the same time. For man and woman differ not only physiologically … but also spiritually and personality-wise. This is the way in which the Creator has ordained human lonely destiny.[8]

Here we find Soloveitchik implicitly relating to the issue of inequality within the marriage relationship. The biblical story of Eve's creation, and the archetypal resonance of that story as the Bible's template for all marriage, appear to imply a hierarchy of man over woman embedded within the very fabric of Creation. The implication is reinforced by the reason given for Eve's necessity, her very purpose: to be an *ezer ke-negdo* (a famously oblique and seemingly paradoxical expression, which nonetheless clearly marks her, in Soloveitchik's term, as a "helper" of some kind) to Adam. Soloveitchik, in a creative interpretive turn, presents the nature of the help Eve is meant to offer as essentially spiritual—indeed, as he repeatedly emphasizes, redemptive—in nature. "The cause of marriage is the exasperating and desolate feeling of loneliness; the purpose of marriage is the redeeming experience of life in fellowship."[9] To achieve this exalted purpose, Soloveitchik seems to argue, requires two fully fleshed-out partners, whose differences do not constitute any form of inequality, but rather to the contrary, serve only to complement each other.

> Because the woman is not a shadow of man but an independent *persona*, because the woman projects a totally different existential image, her companionship helps man to liberate himself from his loneliness. In the interpersonalistic existential tension both man and woman find redemption.[10]

Perhaps Soloveitchik's most powerful theological innovation is to infuse the marriage relationship with a sense of dynamic spiritual drama by imbuing each partner with the dignity of a rich, textured personality and a profound experience of the particularities of their respective, divinely ordained gender identities. The God imagined here is clearly essentialist in His gendered plan for humanity; however, Soloveitchik does evoke, at times with great passion and poetry, a sense of equality, mutuality, and respect within this metaphysical scheme. For example, he notes that Jewish tradition describes marriage using the language of covenant, *brit*, and amplifies the sense of reciprocity implied by that term.

> Apparently, the Bible thinks that the redeeming power of marriage consists in personalizing the sexual experience, in having two strangers, both endowed with equal dignity and worth, meet. And the objective medium of attaining that meeting is the assumption of covenantal obligations which are based on the principle of equality.[11]

Soloveitchik certainly brings a new and nuanced perspective to the traditional Jewish take on marriage. He seems, in these quotations, to accept the moral truth of male/female equality—and then (the apologetic turn) to assert that Judaism upholds this equality, albeit in a novel way that those unfamiliar with the tradition's theological underpinnings might misperceive. Viewed through Soloveitchik's corrective philosophical lens, traditional halakha stands in no need of change; it already embodies the highest aspiration of gender equality, providing a framework for relationships of great spiritual and emotional depth. Without denying the creative boldness of Soloveitchik's enterprise, it is nevertheless here that the essentially defensive posture of his apologetic writing becomes clear.

Halakha and Marriage

Before examining the halakhic treatment of marriage and family life, it might be helpful to conduct a brief thought experiment. Let us suspend any knowledge we may have of various halakhic prescriptions relating to gender and marriage. Working back from Soloveitchik's explanation of the spiritual dynamics of the marital union outlined above, what might we expect the halakha surrounding marriage to look like? If the woman created by God is "not a shadow of man but an independent *persona*," we would expect to see that independence reflected in the halakhic system. If the redemption of marriage depends on, and is constituted by, "having two strangers, both endowed with equal dignity and worth, meet," we would expect to see structural manifestations of that in the halakha as well. If men and women's respective covenantal obligations are indeed "based on the principle of equality," we should find equality as a signature theme emerging from halakhic literature and practice.

And so we begin our examination by asking: According to halakha, what *is* the ground of the relationship of the wife and husband? Is it a sharing of responsibility? A commitment of mutual caring and consideration and love for each other, a respect for the dignity and full personhood of each of the parties, as a more contemporary understanding of the marriage relationship would have it, and as Soloveitchik's explanations would seem to imply? Does the woman have personal independence—the ability to fulfill her own desires?

The weight of evidence from rabbinic material spanning two millennia seems to indicate that the answer to all of these questions is "no."

> A heretic said to Rabban Gamliel, "Your God is a thief! As it is written, 'And God caused a deep sleep to fall upon the human, and he slept' [Gen. 2:21]." Said [Rabban Gamliel's] daughter, "Leave him, for I will answer." She said to the heretic, "Bring

WIN A $100 GIFT CERTIFICATE!

Fill in this card and mail it to us—or fill it in **online** at **jewishlights.com/feedback.html**

—to be eligible for a $100 gift certificate for Jewish Lights books.

JEWISH LIGHTS PUBLISHING
SUNSET FARM OFFICES RTE 4
PO BOX 237
WOODSTOCK VT 05091-0237

Place Stamp Here

Fill in this card and return it to us to be eligible for our quarterly drawing for a $100 gift certificate for Jewish Lights books.

We hope that you will enjoy this book and find it useful in enriching your life.

Book title: _____

Your comments: _____

How you learned of this book: _____

If purchased: Bookseller _____ City _____ State _____

Please send me a free JEWISH LIGHTS Publishing catalog. I am interested in: (check all that apply)

1. ☐ Spirituality
2. ☐ Mysticism/Kabbalah
3. ☐ Philosophy/Theology
4. ☐ History/Politics

5. ☐ Women's Interest
6. ☐ Environmental Interest
7. ☐ Healing/Recovery
8. ☐ Children's Books

9. ☐ Caregiving/Grieving
10. ☐ Ideas for Book Groups
11. ☐ Religious Education Resources
12. ☐ Interfaith Resources

Name (PRINT) _____

Street _____

City _____ State _____ Zip _____

E-MAIL (FOR SPECIAL OFFERS ONLY) _____

Please send a JEWISH LIGHTS Publishing catalog to my friend:

Name (PRINT) _____

Street _____

City _____ State _____ Zip _____

JEWISH LIGHTS PUBLISHING

Tel: (802) 457-4000 • Fax: (802) 457-4004

Available at better booksellers. Visit us online at www.jewishlights.com

me an officer of the law." He said to her, "Why?" "Thieves came upon us last night, took a silver vessel from us, and left a gold one in its place." He said to her, "Would that he would come every day!" *"And was it not favorable to Adam, that God took one rib from him, and gave him a maidservant [shifkha] to serve him?"*

(BT *SANHEDRIN* 39A; EMPHASIS ADDED)

The Talmud seems to record approvingly Rabban Gamliel's daughter's clever, triumphant rebuttal. Her equation of the role of a wife vis-à-vis her husband to that of a slave vis-à-vis her master is implicitly endorsed by the Talmudic editor as expressing a positive cultural value. This imagery represents a different view of marriage than the existential equality offered by Soloveitchik. The creation of Eve from Adam's rib here translates into an ontological subservience, a second-class status inherent in her very reason for being. We might say that this gap is simply a difference of interpretation—Jewish tradition, after all, makes room for multiple opinions—and decide that we prefer Soloveitchik's version. Times have changed, and his existential poetry captures a spiritual and intellectual ambience closer to our own.

Still, a question remains to be asked. Which of these attitudes toward gender and marriage more closely mirrors that found in halakha itself—Soloveitchik's metaphysical community or the Talmud's maidservant? In fact, dominant trends point strongly in the direction of the latter: that the notion of wives as occupying a subservient, "second-class" role in relation to their husbands permeates the halakha's approach to their status in the marriage relationship.

A vivid example of this disparity can be found in one of the central Talmudic tractates dealing with marriage. The Talmud cites a biblical interpretation claiming that while women are obligated in the commandment to "revere" their mother and father—"Every man, you [plural, interpreted as addressing both genders] shall revere your mother and father (Lev. 19:3)"—the verse's odd diction ("every *man*") nevertheless seems to emphasize men's parental obligations more clearly and strongly than women's. The Talmud asks why, then provides its own answer:

> Given that both men and women are required to revere their
> parents, why does Scripture state, "Every *man* ..."? Because it
> is always within a man's capacity to carry out his obligations.
> But it is not always within a woman's capacity to carry out her
> obligations, because [i.e., when she is married] *she is under the*
> *authority of another.*
>
> (BT *KIDDUSHIN* 30B; EMPHASIS ADDED)

Rashi explains: "'*It is always within a man's capacity* ...': No one can pre-
vent him... '*She is under the authority of another*': Her husband." Here
we find clear expression of a fundamental distinction between male
and female status in marriage. If a wife desires to visit her parents, for
example, she requires permission to do so from her husband, while he
bears no reciprocal limitation on his activity. She simply cannot initiate movements on her own without his approval. This halakhic principle is echoed in numerous other areas pertaining to married life. A
young married woman's vow to prohibit upon herself certain items or
actions can be cancelled if the husband is displeased with it. Within
the overall framework of the family, it is he who dominates and
decides, often, the movement and the possibilities that his wife may or
may not undertake.

   While these mores may appear alien, or at least extreme, even to
some modern halakhic observers, it is not incidental to halakha's
approach to and structuring of the institution of marriage. Rather, it
lies at the very core of the halakhic conceptions and prescriptions of
marital roles. The laws governing the terms of how the relationship is
entered into and dissolved—the laws of marriage and divorce—are
structured by halakha in a way that both seems clearly informed by
these imbalanced assumptions and works to reinforce them.

   The Talmud interprets the biblical verse, "If a man takes a woman
and goes into her ..." (Deut. 22:13) to convey exclusive male agency
in initiating and consecrating marriage. The language used is that of
"acquisition." While initially this acquisition could be accomplished
through the conjugal act, the Talmudic Sages instituted that consum-
mation should be preceded by a more formal, contractual affirmation

of the union: a marriage document and/or the presentation of an item of value, customarily a ring. The late thirteenth-century commentator Rabbi Pinchas Halevi of Barcelona offers an explanation for why the Rabbis instituted these formal legal mechanisms:

> In order that she should realize in her heart forever that she is acquired by that man. That she should not commit immorality under him, nor rebel against him, but should pay him honor and homage forever after, *as a servant does his master.* [emphasis added][12]

The motif of male agency and female passivity finds even stronger expression in the halakha pertaining to divorce, whose enacting requires voluntary action *only* on the part of the husband. The wife can neither initiate a divorce nor reject it. The Talmudic Rabbis base their prescriptions in this area on an interpretation of a sequence of verses in Deuteronomy.

> A man takes a wife and possesses her. She fails to please him because he finds something obnoxious about her, and he writes her a bill of divorcement, hands it to her, and sends her away from his house; she leaves his household and becomes the wife of another man; then this latter man rejects her, writes her a bill of divorcement, hands it to her, and sends her away from his house; or the man who married her last dies. Then the first husband who divorced her shall not take her to wife again, since she has been defiled—for that would be abhorrent to the Lord. You must not bring sin upon the land that the Lord your God is giving you as a heritage.
>
> (DEUT. 24:1–4)

The main thrust of these verses seems to treat the legal case of whether a woman who has divorced two men (or divorced one and become widowed by the second) may return to the first. The Talmudic Rabbis employed midrashic tools of interpretation to infer, from the language

used, the foundational rules of divorce procedure. Maimonides sum-
marizes their discussion and encodes it as law:

> The following ten things are essential to constitute a *get* accord-
> ing to the Torah: (1) That a man should only divorce according
> to his own will ... and from where in the Torah do we derive
> these ten principles? As it is written, "[...] then it comes to
> pass, if she find no favor in his eyes ... that he write her a bill
> of divorcement, and give it in her hand, and send her out of his
> house" (Deut. 24:1). "If she find no favor in his eyes"—this
> teaches that he only divorces according to his will; and if she
> divorces [i.e., attempts to divorce] him against his will, she is
> not divorced. But the woman is divorced whether according to
> her will or against her will.[13]

These foundational frames of reference for traditional Judaism's
understanding of the role of the woman in marriage—as
Maimonides mentions, their authority is seen as deriving from the
Torah itself, and indeed they have remained authoritative, and
mostly unchanged, to this day—do not seem to reflect Soloveitchik's
metaphysical mutuality or any number of other modern apologetic
assertions about the spiritual-psychological dimension of Jewish
marriage. This, indeed, is what gives them the name "apologetics" in
the first place: while we may acknowledge in them sparks of theological creativity, at heart these are conservative, defensive postures
designed to appease a more contemporary moral sensibility and bolster the tradition's moral credibility without actually changing
halakhic practice in any way. It is this kind of intellectual games-
manship that gives apologetics their connotation of bad faith.

Soloveitchik's passionate and poetic characterization of the marriage relationship breaks down when confronted with halakhic reality.
The halakha prescribing marital roles has been mediated by a different
spirit, a different image of the biblical God than the one appropriated
by Soloveitchik, who "thinks that the redeeming power of marriage
consists in personalizing the sexual experience, in having two

strangers, both endowed with equal dignity and worth, meet." The Rabbis were not abashed about describing this other spirit, praising its wisdom and attributing it to divine decree ("And was it not favorable to Adam, that God took one rib from him, and gave him a maidservant [*shifkha*] to serve him?").

In fact, for rabbis throughout Jewish history, gender inequality has been a point of pride, a mechanism enshrined by God in the fabric of His universe—and thus naturally in His revealed halakha—to ensure domestic harmony for His Chosen People. Rabbi Pinchas Halevi, in the continuation of the passage quoted above justifying the mechanisms of halakhic marital "acquisition," praises God in just this way as he echoes and amplifies the Talmudic "maidservant" motif: "That she should not commit immorality under him, nor rebel against him, but should pay him honor and homage forever after as a servant does his master. *Thereby their life together will be in peace forever after, and the settled community will endure with the will of God, who desires it*" [emphasis added].[14]

Rabbi Pinchas Halevi is theologically consistent when he comes to explain the reason for the gender imbalance embedded within divorce law:

> At the root of this precept lies the reason that a woman was created to be as a helper to a man, and she is to him as one of his cherished instruments—in keeping with what the Sages of blessed memory said: A woman does not plight her troth (bind herself in covenant) to any but the one who makes an "instrument" of her. Well, since it is so, it is His will (blessed be He) that at any time one's spirit becomes repelled by this instrument, he may remove it from his house … since she is to him no more than as a precious instrument in the house. [emphasis added][15]

Like Rabbi Soloveitchik, Rabbi Pinchas Halevi ties his understanding of the fundamental gender dynamic within marriage to an interpretation of the biblical description of woman's creation by God as a

"helper" to man. The images of God that inform their respective interpretations are quite disparate. But it is Rabbi Pinchas's version that
finds halakhic expression in the laws of marriage and divorce.

Halakhic Woman: Nurturing Servant

The conception of women's roles vis-à-vis their husbands reflected in
marriage and divorce law forms the basis of a broader halakhic conception of the female role within the family—which, as we shall soon see,
becomes definitional to her very identity as a creature of God. As a "servant" of her husband, halakha relegates the wife to the near-exclusive
role of caregiver/nurturer, to him and to the children they have together.

This attitude finds paradigmatic expression in the dominant
Talmudic understanding of women's "standing" with respect to the
study of Torah. In Deuteronomy, Moses commands a communal
assembly to take place every seventh year in Jerusalem, at which the
Torah is read in a massive celebratory reaffirmation ceremony.

> When all Israel comes to appear before the Lord your God in
> the place that He will choose, you shall read this Teaching
> aloud in the presence of all Israel. Gather the people—men,
> women, children, and the strangers in your communities—
> that they may hear and so learn to revere the Lord your God
> and to observe faithfully every word of this Teaching.
>
> (DEUT. 31:11–12)

The spirit of inclusiveness and even equality regarding access to God's
word that emerges from the biblical text seems to have run counter to
certain aspects of Talmudic theology and/or sociology. The following
midrash on these verses is reported to have been expounded publicly
by Rabbi Elazar ben Azariah, the leading sage of his generation:

> "Assemble the people, the men and the women and the small
> children" (Deut. 31:11): If the men come to learn, and the
> woman come to hear, why do the small children come? In
> order to give a reward to those who bring them.
>
> (BT HAGIGAH 3B)

For Rabbi Elazar ben Azariah, the woman's role is to listen, but not to learn. She is a passive receiver and nurturer. For the kind of informal, motherly teaching for which she is responsible, real intellectual engagement is not necessary; a more superficial "hearing," along with the merit accrued by bringing the children, suffices. The Talmud takes this case as paradigmatic and extends it into a broad social norm:

> Rav said to Rav Hiyah: By virtue of what deeds do women merit reward? By taking their children to the classroom, by sending their husbands to the house of study, and by waiting for them until they return.
>
> (BT BERACHOT 17A)

For the Rabbis, women are, *by design*, not shapers of culture, for this would impinge upon their capacity to serve their husbands and families, thus transgressing their essential purpose and role. Like the midrashic image of the matriarch Sara, filling her familial dwelling with the soft Sabbath candlelight—"Sara ... in the tent" (Gen. 18:9) having been inscribed by the Sages as an archetype of the traditional female role—the job of the halakhic woman is most importantly to be available to serve the needs of her husband and family.[16] This is consistent with the tradition's understanding of the verse describing the first woman as, first and foremost, a "helper" to man; the Talmud's read on "helper" as "maidservant," and Pinchas Halevi's related extension of the biblical term to mean "instrument."

It is this imagery around which the halakha of marriage was formed. It is also the imagery around which the ideals of marriage are framed and perpetuated within many halakhic communities. A Talmudic story that vividly captures one dimension of this ideal concerns the relationship between Rabbi Akiva and his wife. Akiva came to Judaism late in life, according to the Talmud, and proceeded to become one of the greatest Torah scholars of all time. This feat was accomplished in large part because his wife encouraged him to leave their home and study full-time in a remote Talmudic academy for twelve years. After that time, he returned to his home with twelve thousand disciples following him. He overheard a neighbor saying to his wife, "How long will you live as a married widow? Your husband has totally forgotten you!" "If he would listen to me," Akiva's wife answered, "he should go study another twelve years." Akiva took this as approval and left immediately to commence another twelve years of study. The story culminates with Akiva admonishing his students, "What both I and you have is hers."

When I studied in Lakewood, this story was often referenced as the type of marital relationship to which all serious yeshiva students and their wives must aspire. I was admonished by more than one rabbi, on more than one occasion, to study the story with my wife, so that she might understand what her true role in marriage was about, what her greatest achievement as a spouse could be: to negate her relational needs and desires so that I, her husband, might have a chance to become the biggest Torah scholar that I could be.

Lofty Language, Rigid Roles: Is Gender Inequality Merely "Torah-Tolerated"?

Notwithstanding the deep frameworks of gender imbalance encoded within the halakhic system, rabbinic tradition also contains voices urging the positive treatment of wives. Among the most well-known of these is found in Maimonides's "Laws of Marriage," in which he describes how a husband should behave toward his wife:

> A husband should not be overly jealous of his wife; nor should he coerce her, and force her to have sex against her will, but only with her agreement, and amid conversation and joy…. So too, the Sages commanded that a man should honor his wife more than himself, and love her as he loves his own body; and if he has money, to use it to increase her benefit. And he should not cast an excess of fear over her; and his speech with her should be gentle, and neither sad nor angry.[17]

This passage is often quoted in apologetic arguments wishing to refute the claim that the tradition holds a negative attitude toward women. How do we understand this statement and others like it in light of the discussion above? Eliezer Berkowitz, one of the only modern halakhic thinkers to acknowledge the moral issues of halakhic gender categories, sees it as evidence of a halakhic system in an ongoing process of ethical self-correction with respect to women's status. To describe this process, Berkowitz develops a theory of halakhic development that distinguishes between laws that are "Torah-tolerated" and those that are "Torah-established," "Torah-directed," or "Torah-taught":

> There were essentially three distinct phases in the evolving status of Jewish women. The first phase was Torah-tolerated rather than Torah-established or Torah-taught. It derived from the mores, conditions, and circumstances of an early age, and was not essentially different from what we find in other societies at the same stage of development. Women's status in this era was nonpersonal. While it could not be changed overnight by legislation, certain limited changes were effected to indicate the direction of the kind of development the Torah desired.[18]

For Berkowitz, Jewish tradition exists in a constant tug-of-war between general, inherited societal mores and the drive toward moral perfection, which is, in his view, the Torah's ultimate purpose. Thus, he grants that the tradition holds many negative statements and laws with respect to women. But he claims that alongside them there also developed a tradition with a more positive attitude toward women, out of which grew a series of halakhic innovations that demonstrate the true end goal the Torah wishes us to pursue. The direction within the tradition, he says, moves toward an increasing acknowledgment of women as "personal" (i.e., autonomous to themselves) rather than "impersonal" (i.e., instrumental to others).

> The fact that the negative opinions about Jewish women were not unanimous indicates that there was another source determining

women's status. Much was Torah-tolerated, but there was also Torah-guidance.... The method of the Torah is to acknowledge reality, to take human nature into account and to apply the eternal word to it so far as is possible. Thus to teach values and guide behavior, indicating the goal towards which guided change has to move. The goal is to integrate the eternal with the temporal.[19]

Berkowitz quotes the passage from Maimonides above about how husbands should treat their wives and contrasts it with the parallel description about how wives are required to treat their husbands. This contrast, for him, presents a classic example of the way in which different, seemingly conflicting or competitive voices—remnants from social worlds the Torah would prefer we transcend, alongside the voices advancing the Torah's true moral priorities—coexist uneasily within the tradition. "Nothing shows this more convincingly than the way in which Maimonides combined some essential features of the personal and impersonal status"[20] than his juxtaposition of husbandly responsibilities with those of the wife:

> And thus have our Sages commanded upon the woman, that she remain modestly within her home, and not overly indulge in joking and frivolity in front of her husband; and not ask him verbally for sex; and not speak about this matter; and not refuse her husband, tormenting him so that his love will increase; but she should be willing, whenever he wants.... And so too have our Sages commanded upon the woman that she honor her husband "more than enough," that the fear of him should be upon her, and that all her work should be done in accordance with his instruction; he should be in her eyes like a prince or a king who may act as he desires; she should also remove before him everything that is hateful to him, etc.[21]

Berkowitz cannot understand how, in one voice, Maimonides says that a man should respect his wife as much as him and more, and treat her gently and kindly; and combine that, in the same series of rulings, with a law that the wife should always be available to the husband and view him as a king and master. How can these two images stand side by side?

> It is difficult to understand why Maimonides did not see the contradiction between these two commands. How can a husband who loves and honors his wife, as indicated, want her to fear him, to look up at him as if he were a prince simply because he happens to be her husband, and to remove from his presence everything that might displease him? The truth is that the two principles are mutually exclusive: either you love your wife as yourself and honor her more than yourself, or you demand that she regard you as her lord and master, and serve you accordingly.[22]

For Berkowitz, the true direction of Torah is to see women as dignified and autonomous beings, and not only as instruments of their husbands. But while I admire his ethical sensitivity, I do not share his surprise or sense of contradiction between these two statements of Maimonides. This difference speaks to a broader critique of his "Torah-tolerated" versus "Torah-directed" framework. In Berkowitz's theology, halakha is an *essentially* moral and progressive mechanism. Because the Torah, for him, is inherently moral, all traces of immorality within it must be traced to an outside source. What Berkowitz fails or refuses to face, in my opinion, is the extent to which halakha, both its practitioners and shapers throughout history, have embraced gender inequality as an ideal unto itself (see above, e.g., Rabbi Pinchas Halevi). By clinging to the belief in the tradition's essential morality, which is far from self-evident, he seems to blind himself to the possibility that the halakhic system might be operating zealously, systematically, and on its own terms righteously, to keep women circumscribed within the roles understood to have been allocated them by God.

While Berkowitz claims to trace an evolution of women's status within halakha from "impersonal" to "personal" and notes some important halakhic innovations in support of this point, as demonstrated above, it is difficult to find ways in which the halakhic edifice with respect to women has been fundamentally changed. Marriage and divorce laws that enshrine this imbalance remain active. The image of God that has informed and controlled the halakhic development of women's status around the vast majority of relevant issues has been the one that praises His benevolence in creating a nurturing, subservient "helper" for man.

It is hard to understand how Berkowitz can see Talmudic misogyny as merely Torah-tolerated when we see how zealously the Sages embraced Roman and Greek views and mores with respect to women. They felt that in doing so they were speaking the spirit of Torah. They didn't believe that they were tolerating these things; they embraced them as representing the ideal type of relationship between man and woman. This is the direction in which they were directing the Torah. They were very satisfied with this relational framework. By not acknowledging a moral critique of the tradition, Berkowitz has convinced himself that halakha is essentially moral. I fundamentally question both the truth of, and the need for, this claim. It is possible to morally correct the tradition without making claims of moral purity.

Thus, I believe that these two images within Maimonides's marital prescriptions can be easily reconciled when we consider the requirements, under Torah law, of a master with respect to a slave. This is not to claim that the status of a woman is halakhically identical to that of a slave. But it is to point out that her status may be closer to that of a slave than of, say, a good friend or business partner. The kind, even excessively attentive treatment that the Torah mandates and exhorts masters to extend to their slaves does not weaken the essential power imbalance or mitigate the latter's essentially subservient status. Rules of ethical behavior toward slaves and wives do not alter the authoritarian grounds of the relationship.

Berkowitz is deeply aware that much found in the Talmud regarding the wife's role in the family has its roots in the framework of the Greek and Roman culture within which they were formed. It is worth noting that Greek and Roman culture also urged good treatment toward women without giving them equal status. Thus, while I admire Berkowitz's ethical sensitivity and courage, ultimately his categories fall short of acknowledging the depth of the moral breakdown of the tradition's approach to women's status in marriage. They do not touch the core issue of the passive role of the woman in the family, the fundamental asymmetry of the spousal relationship, and the lengths to which the representatives of the tradition have gone to celebrate and uphold it. Her life is guided by his will. As long as that framework is kept in existence—not tolerated but established, directed, and taught—by halakhic communities, it seems unlikely that any real solution toward the gender issue will be found.

Women and Ritual Life

The image of the woman as the nurturing servant of the husband and children embedded in marriage/divorce law becomes the structuring motif, halakhically, of her identity; all other relationships are organized around it. This includes her relationship to God. As shown above, halakha limits women to a more remote and superficial access to the primary channel of God's word, Torah study. As spiritual creatures, their essential "reward"—another way of designating their purpose—is achieved through, and thus defined by, the fulfillment of their supporting role: "By taking their children to the classroom, by sending their husbands to the house of study, and by waiting for them until they return" (BT *Berachot* 17a).

Halakhically, the exemption of women from Torah study segregates them into what might almost be considered a separate spiritual caste. It is not only that lacking direct access to the mechanisms of culture (i.e., the sacred tradition), women within traditional Judaism may never become active creators of culture. There is also the internal religious dimension, being deprived of exposure to the vehicles of personal and collective spiritual growth. Women within this framework cannot be initiators, conquerors, or builders—even of themselves.

The diminished spiritual valuation reflected in the absence of an obligation to study Torah correlates to a diminished level of responsibility in the sphere of mitzvot. It only takes the Talmud two short interpretive steps to extrapolate the latter from the former. Since the commandment to wear tefillin concludes with what the Talmudic Rabbis understood as a reference connecting its purpose to Torah study—"And this shall serve you as a sign on your hand and as a reminder on your forehead—*in order that the Teaching of the Lord may be in your mouth*" (Exod. 13:9; emphasis added)—they extended this reasoning into a ruling that women are exempt from the mitzvah of tefillin as well (*Mekhilta*, Tractate *Pischa*, 17). This in turn serves as the basis for a blanket exemption from all positive, time-bound mitzvot:

> Just as women are exempt from wearing tefillin, so too are they exempt from all positive, time-bound mitzvot.... Scripture states, "And this shall serve you as a sign on your hand and a reminder between your eyes *in order that the Teachings of the Lord may be in your mouth*" (Exod. 13:9; emphasis added). Thus, the entire Torah is compared to tefillin. Just as tefillin is a positive, time-bound mitzvah, so too are all women exempt from all positive, time-bound mitzvot.
>
> (BT *KIDDUSHIN* 34A)

The Talmud provides no logical basis for the associative connection between tefillin and "the entire Torah," but rather presents it as an implicit assumption or received tradition. In the interim, various commentators have attempted to fill in this interpretive gap. One such attempt can be found in a fourteenth-century commentary on synagogue liturgy, known as the *Abudarham*, which remains popular among religious Jews to this day:

> Woman is exempt from positive, time-bound mitzvot because she is bound to her husband to attend to his needs. Were a woman obliged to perform such mitzvot, her husband might bid her to do something at the precise moment she is fulfilling one of these mitzvot. Should she fulfill the bidding of her Creator and neglect her husband's demands, she faces her hus-

band's wrath. On the other hand, should she fulfill her husband's demands and neglect the bidding of her Creator, she faces the wrath of her Creator. Consequently, the Creator exempted her from these obligations in order to promote harmony between husband and wife.[23]

Here we find ourselves again on familiar ground; the *Abudarham* is clearly drawing upon a rich and widespread tradition. Women cannot participate fully in the spiritual life of mitzvot in general for precisely the same reason they cannot be fully obligated in the mitzvah of parental reverence discussed above: because of its potential to bring her into conflict with her primary purpose and role, attending to her husband as a nurturing servant. Here, as there, "the authority of others" weighs decisively upon any consideration she may entertain. Here, as there, the marginalization of all other relationships for the sake of exalting the husband's regal authority over her is framed theologically as a source of gratitude and a point of pride—a gift of divine benevolence, an extra measure of God's wisdom bequeathed to the Jewish community: "Consequently, the Creator exempted her from these obligations in order to promote harmony between husband and wife." Here again we find that the gender imbalance embedded within the halakhic system has been embraced, by some of its most authoritative practitioners, as ethically positive and divinely inspired.

Based upon this principle of family harmony, women have been exempted, and thus excluded, from virtually any active role in establishing the collective ritual worship life in the synagogue. They are not counted in the traditional prayer quorum; they do not stand for the community as prayer leaders; they do not read publicly from the Torah. Since the Enlightenment, this discrepancy has been met by skepticism and criticism by liberal, and later feminist, thinkers. Since that time, some modern Orthodox rabbis have acknowledged the gender discrepancy within the ritual sphere—implicitly affirming its underlying egalitarian assumptions—and responding with different forms of apologetics. Generally speaking, they tend to offer explanations of women's diminished ritual role that present it as reflecting something positive about their essential nature. A classic example of this genre was advanced by Rabbi Samson Raphael Hirsch, a founding figure of modern Orthodoxy in nineteenth-century Germany:

> Clearly, women's exemption from positive, time-bound mitzvot is not a consequence of their diminished worth; nor is it because the Torah found them unfit, as it were, to fulfill these mitzvot. Rather, it seems to me, it is because the Torah understood that women are not in need of these mitzvot. The Torah affirms that our women are imbued with a great love and a holy enthusiasm for their role in divine worship, exceeding that of man. The trials men undergo in their professional activities jeopardize their fidelity to Torah, and therefore they require from time to time reminders and warnings in the form of time-bound mitzvot. Women, whose lifestyle does not subject them to comparable trials and hazards, have no need for such periodic reminders.[24]

Rabbi Hirsch combines ontological ("our women are imbued with a great love and holy enthusiasm") and sociopsychological ("the trials men undergo in their professional activities jeopardize their fidelity to Torah") factors to construct a more ethically palatable understanding of women's exemption/exclusion from positive, time-bound mitzvot. His stance is theologically striking inasmuch as it takes the traditional interpretation of women's mitzvah exemption and flips it on its head: it is not because women are less valued than men; it is because they are *more* valued. This radical reframing of the traditional attitude toward women reflects the extent of Hirsch's sensitivity to the ethical critique of traditional Judaism's marginalization of women in the ritual sphere. His humble tone ("it seems to me ...") may also reflect an acknowledgment that he is not speaking in the name of received tradition but rather offering a new and novel way of understanding it. Nevertheless, his ultimate intent is clearly to justify halakha in light of the egalitarian critique, not to transform it.

No such hesitancy of tone is found in the more contemporary, comprehensive, and openly polemical apologetics of Rabbi Aaron Soloveitchik (whom, for the sake of clarity to distinguish him from his brother, Rabbi Joseph B. Soloveitchik, quoted above, I will refer to henceforth as A. Soloveitchik). Unlike Hirsch, A. Soloveitchik did not merely have the egalitarian critique offered by liberal philosophy to contend with, but the more radical and systemic claims of modern feminism—and, even more importantly, the liberal Jewish movements that accepted them—against halakha. According to A. Soloveitchik, the feminist critique of traditional Judaism amounts to a giant misunderstanding, and he sees his role as clarifying the ignorant misconceptions upon which it is based:

> Unfortunately, many people nowadays misunderstand the Torah's view of the role of the woman. They cite laws and blessings which they claim, in their ignorance, reflect an attitude of, God forbid, disdain for the woman. It is therefore incumbent upon us to present the Torah's true attitude towards the difference in gender.[25]

A. Soloveitchik's aggressive rhetoric may reflect a genuine horror at the suggestion he so totally rejects. Having known him personally, I remember Rabbi Aaron Soloveitchik as a sweet and highly moral, even saintly, man. From all that is known of him, he loved his wife deeply and treated her with great affection and respect. The notion that the Torah, his other great love, might be seen as disrespecting her, as he understood feminism to claim, clearly provoked his passions. In response, he begins by discussing a well-known midrash assigning to the "righteous women" who lived in the time of the Exodus credit for the Jewish people's redemption from slavery in Egypt. Paraphrasing and building on this theme, he poses the rhetorical question, "What did the women do at the critical moment to ensure the redemption of the Jewish people?"

> They strengthened the men, inspiring them to courageous endurance, cultivating their spirit, and providing in their lives

that dedicated atmosphere which rendered it possible for them to persevere and to find an essential modicum of Divine sweetness and joy, which more than atoned for their sorrows and trials.[26]

From this midrash, A. Soloveitchik draws two broad inferences: (1) "Judaism not only accords to the woman an encomium of appreciation as an equal partner of the man," but (2) "it also recognizes the feminine gender as possessing an innate, unique spiritual blessing as compared with the male gender."[27] Here we find something akin to the "separate-but-equal" theology advanced by Joseph B. Soloveitchik above, an acknowledgment of women and men's ontological difference that presents this difference as complementary and thus "equal," rather than hierarchical. Indeed, if anything, A. Soloveitchik extends the theological kernel found in Hirsch into the radical claim that women's exemption from mitzvot reflects a spiritual *advantage* over men, a holy spark unique to their feminine nature. Not surprisingly, he grounds this understanding in a midrashic reading of the biblical creation narrative:

This outlook can be deduced from a mere cursory glance at the Creation in Genesis. It appears from Genesis that whatever is superior was created later: "... the world was created with ten Divine decrees" [*Pirkei Avot* 5:1]. First light was created and with it other forms of energy; then the inorganic world and then the organic world. And in the organic world, vegetative life came first and then animal life. And again, in the animal kingdom, the lower species came first and then the higher species. Adam, humankind, was created after all animals. In the human species, the male gender came first and then the female gender. This proves the proposition that the woman has innate spiritual advantage as compared with man.[28]

The forced offhandedness with which A. Soloveitchik presents his reading ("a mere cursory glance ...") is perhaps a way of rhetorically downplaying its extreme theological novelty: Women are not their husbands' servants; nor are they merely full, equal partners. They are, in fact, higher beings—a window into the direction of human spiritual progress. A. Soloveitchik constructs an innovative theological dialectic that identifies men with the ontological quality of "conquest" and women with that of "cultivation." He is careful to emphasize both that "these two blessings represent two different gifts or approaches, two distinct endowments"[29] and that this scheme represents an expression of divine wisdom and benevolence. "God the Creator formed man and woman with different constitutions, not only biologically and physically, but especially psychologically, emotionally and spiritually."[30]

On one level, A. Soloveitchik is clearly sensitive and responsive to the moral claims of gender equality. However, his faith in a particular notion of halakhic purity and unchangeability cannot allow him to see or acknowledge the ways in which halakha has, indeed, been shaped by an active embrace of gender inequality. Instead of facing halakhic reality, he seeks refuge in theological creativity, developing a new way of talking about gender that attempts to justify halakhic practice in spiritual and moral terms in order to bolster its moral credentials against critique and, ultimately, the possibility of change.

For A. Soloveitchik, the failure of modern critics of halakha to grasp "The Torah's true attitude towards the difference in gender" amounts to an almost willful ignorance, with which he not infrequently grows impatient. This impatience seems somewhat ironic in light of the originality of A. Soloveitchik's theology; how could anyone understand it before reading it in his pages? His distinctly modern point of view cannot be found within traditional sources. Nevertheless, he sharply rebukes those who might see, for example, halakha's exemption of women from positive, time-bound mitzvot as reflecting a negative attitude toward women within the tradition:

> Many self-crowned enlightened people conjure up the erroneous
> notion that Judaism considers and treats the woman as inferior
> to man. In order to corroborate this proposition, these so-called
> enlightened people mention the fact that the Torah exempts

women from obligatory mitzvot created by a time element [i.e., positive, time-bound mitzvot], as well as from Torah study.[31]

A. Soloveitchik places the question on his theological axis of "conquest" versus "cultivation" and comes up with a creative interpretation of these gender discrepancies:

> God imposed more mitzvot upon the man than upon the woman because a man is innately disposed towards excessive and abusive *kibbush* (conquest), grasping. There is a natural abundance of energy in the male gender which, if not tempered and controlled properly, can be released in a very destructive manner. God, in His infinite wisdom, therefore imposed upon the male gender the positive, time-bound mitzvot and the obligation of constantly being engaged in the study of Torah so that man's psyche will always be preoccupied with spiritual and intellectual endeavors, thereby counteracting man's natural disposition towards abusive *kibbush* (conquest).[32]

On a similar note, A. Soloveitchik takes on those critics who note the discrepancy in the form of the blessings halakha prescribes for men and women, respectively, upon awakening in the morning:

> They also mention the fact that whereas every morning a man recites the blessing "[Blessed are You, Lord our God, King of the Universe,] who has not made me a woman," a woman recites, "[Blessed are You, Lord our God, King of the Universe,] who has made me according to his desire."[33]

His response is theologically consistent, and yet so bold that it merits quoting in full. The reason men thank God for not having made them women, and women thank God for making them as they are, is not a statement of men's theological priority over women, but very much the opposite. It is, in fact, the same reason that God endowed women with fewer mitzvot in the first place:

Such restrictive mandates were not imposed upon woman. A woman recites the *bracha* of "… who has made me according to his desire," not because of lesser innate qualities but, rather, because the innate qualities of woman, the last created creature, the crown of Creation, are already bent toward the future culmination of God's desire. A man has to struggle in order to be compassionate, tolerant, and noble. A woman's personality was molded by the Creator in such a way that she is naturally endowed or disposed toward compassion and consideration. The very word equivalent in the Hebrew language to compassion is *rachmanus*, from *rechem*, meaning a woman's womb.[34]

Ingeniously, A. Soloveitchik acknowledges the gender discrepancy within traditional Judaism, then claims that the discrepancy actually favors women. The study of Torah and the practice of mitzvot are framed as spiritual tools designed to help curb man's—specifically *man's*—baser instincts. Women, lacking such instincts, find themselves without need for such tools. While men were given mitzvot and Torah study to toil in for the purpose, he almost seems to suggest, of "keeping them off the streets," women embody a progressive vision of human potential and purpose.

> Women's character was molded by God in accordance with the eschatological goals that God reserved for the world. In the Messianic Era, every human being will be pursuing the gift of *chazakah* (cultivation), reaching. There will be no pursuit of *kibbush* (conquest), grasping. Consequently, a woman recites the blessing of "… who has made me according to His desire." This blessing, far from implying a negative attitude towards the woman, is actually expressive of the positive status of the woman in the Torah's view. Its intent is that a woman's Divine endowment, her very nature, is in accordance with the Divine attributes of compassion, tolerance, and grace. Woman's endowment, and therefore her mandate to be true to that endowment, accords with the spiritual and moral trend of humanity in the Messianic era.[35]

A. Soloveitchik's understanding of women's status within halakha is founded overtly, even insistently, on a particular image of God. This is a God who has formulated essential gender roles for men and for women in order to channel certain energies built into the fundamental dynamic of Creation, moving humanity ever closer to its divinely ordained destiny: "Women's character was molded by God in accordance with the eschatological goals that God reserved for the world."

Without delving into an analysis of the various examples and interpretations A. Soloveitchik enlists in support of his dialectical gender theology, let it suffice to say this: whatever its theological merits, it is difficult to find the God he evokes mirrored within the fundamental halakhic structures we have examined. If women are indeed the enlightened creatures A. Soloveitchik claims Jewish tradition holds them to be, why are they deprived agency while entering, leaving, and living within marriage? Shouldn't they be the ones determining whether their husbands' desires for personal movement and spiritual development (and, as we shall soon see, public involvement as well) are reasonable and worthwhile, and not the other way around? Shouldn't they have the freedom and dignity to decide how their life's priorities should be balanced, without fearing this will lead to an inevitable rift in the bedrock of the family structure? Indeed, if we recall the midrash A. Soloveitchik uses to support his claim that the tradition valorizes women, we will see that even in doing so it locates them squarely in a secondary, supporting role:

> They strengthened the men, inspiring them to courageous endurance, cultivating their spirit, and providing in their lives that dedicated atmosphere which rendered it possible for them to persevere and to find an essential modicum of Divine sweetness and joy, which more than atoned for their sorrows and trials.[36]

The claim that this supporting role, because of its instrumental importance to Jewish community—echoing the motif of women's self-negation for the sake of "family harmony" discussed above—

somehow amounts to "equal" status with men is belied by a halakhic system that denies them autonomy. However sincere the esteem in which A. Soloveitchik may have held his wife, and women generally, the essential halakhic structures governing their lives give voice to a different spirit and a far less elevated status than his theology would seem to mandate.

Hirsch, writing two centuries earlier about the same problematic blessing, seemed to recognize that the evidence from the tradition allowed for far more modest claims about its meaning for the women obligated to say it. His explanation argues not that the blessing "… who made me according to His desire" reflects an attitude of female superiority, but something closer to an attitude of resigned non-inferiority:

> This is not a prayer of thanks that God did not make us heathens, slaves, or women. Rather, it calls upon us to contemplate the task which God has imposed upon us by making us free Jewish men, and to pledge ourselves to do justice to this mission. These three aspects of our own status impose upon us duties much more comprehensive than those required of the rest of mankind. And if our women have a smaller number of mitzvoth to fulfill than men, they know that the tasks which they must discharge as free Jewish women are no less in accordance with the will and desire of God than are those of their brothers.[37]

For Hirsch, mitzvot are still a precious divine gift whose bestowal enhances—rather than, as in A. Soloveitchik's version, diminishes—the spiritual status of their recipient. They are not a remedy to moral deprivation, but a rather heroic "task which God has imposed upon us by making us free Jewish men." This association of mitzvot with heroism leaves Hirsch with far less room to negotiate the moral implications of women's more meager inheritance. His indirect, negative formulation ("they know that the tasks which they must discharge as free Jewish women are *no less* in accordance with the will and desire of

God"; emphasis added) suggests that he is offering this interpretation as a kind of consolation prize, a comfort to the women of his day, the intellectual merits of which even he is not fully convinced.

Earlier interpretations of the genesis and meaning of this blessing—along with its male counterpart, "... who did not make me a woman"—openly embrace the gender imbalance it seems, on its surface, to express. The Talmudic mind-set could hardly be clearer than when it earnestly ponders the possible redundancy of thanking God for being created neither a slave *nor* a woman.[38] "What form do the morning blessings take? '... who has not made me a slave.' *Is not a slave equivalent to a woman?*" [i.e., shouldn't the "slave" blessing include, conceptually, the "woman" blessing, obviating its need] (BT *Menachot* 43b; emphasis added). Rashi, explaining the Talmud's equation of women and slaves in this passage, amplifies what is by now a familiar motif: "For a woman is a 'slave' to her husband as a slave is to his master" (Rashi, BT *Menachot* 43b).

Rabbi Yaakov ben Asher, author of the seminal halakhic work the *Tur*, codifies a similar spirit in his explanation of the women's version of the traditional blessing: "Women initiated the custom of saying '... who made me according to His will.' It is possible that she behaves this way as someone who justifies the judgment of an evil decree" (Heb. *tziduk ha-din*; *Tur, Orach Hayim*, 46). In this understanding of the blessing's intent, the woman who pronounces it bemoans her fate, while at the same time justifying God's unfathomable, but painful, judgment. It is a version of what is said upon learning of a death, and the same spirit in which the *Kaddish* is chanted. The woman experiences her very being under the harsh, tragic judgment of God, while recognizing that it is a fate she must obediently accept.

Both Hirsch and A. Soloveitchik were certainly familiar with the traditions quoted above, all of which are found within works still universally studied among traditional Jews. In this light, the harsh derision A. Soloveitchik, in particular, directs at those critical of women's reduced status within halakha (his primary implicit targets being contemporary Reform and Conservative rabbis) begins to take on an air of absurdity:

> Many self-crowned enlightened people conjure up the erroneous notion that Judaism considers and treats the woman as inferior to man ... these so-called enlightened people ... so-called Jewish leaders who do not subjugate themselves to the authority of Torah....[39]

In light of a clear system of precedents within the tradition leading to this very conclusion, we can only wonder if A. Soloveitchik would have applied the same dismissive epithets to the Mishnaic authors who decreed, "A man takes precedence over a woman to sustain [literally, 'to keep alive'] and to return a lost object ... and if both are in danger, a man's life take precedence to save" (*Mishnah Horayot* 3:7)—or, for that matter, to Maimonides, who explains women's lesser value precisely in the context of their exclusion from mitzvot and Torah study. Maimonides takes care to note that this value discrepancy is constitutive of the male and female genders and cannot be remedied, for example, by voluntary action:

> A woman who has studied Torah receives reward. However, it is not like the reward a man receives, because she is not commanded. And anyone who does something that is not commanded upon him, his reward is not like the reward of the commanded one who does it, but rather less. Moreover, even though she receives reward, the Sages commanded that a man should not teach his daughter Torah. Because most women's minds are not capable of conceptual learning, and they turn Torah into nonsense, due to their mental poverty. As the Sages said: Anyone who teaches his daughter Torah, teaches her licentiousness.[40]

Is Maimonides one of the "self-crowned enlightened people" who "conjure up the erroneous notion that Judaism considers and treats the woman as inferior to man"? A. Soloveitchik's sincere belief in the positive role of women in halakha may have reflected his marital relationship and his own moral nature. Neither of these, however, serves as a credible basis for representing, as he does in his chapter title, "The Torah's View of the Role of the Woman." He cannot enlist the authority of God and Torah as the exclusive word on the subject of gender relationships in Judaism. Indeed, the more stridently he pleads this case, the sharper its contradictions and embarrassing ironies start to seem. His exaltation of pious Jewish women for their role in liberating our ancestors from Egypt does nothing to mitigate the spirit of servitude that informs much of the halakha within which they live. To the contrary, his polemical purpose is to ensure that these structures remain firmly, eternally, in place.

Women and the Public Life of the Community

By this point in the discussion, traditional halakha's response to the notion of women's participation in public life should be fairly obvious. The normative motif of "family harmony" rules here as well, with its relegation of women to the home, to their capacity as nurturer of husband and children, to the exclusion of any other priorities, interests, and desires.

This spirit is elaborated and codified in halakhic sources that systemically disqualify women from taking on roles of public responsibility, which would give them a voice in shaping the values and direction of communal life. These are sources with deep, authoritative roots in the Rabbinic canon. One of the most significant must be seen as the Talmud's disqualification of women from serving as witnesses for nearly any official purpose (BT *Shevuot* 30a). Women cannot act as signatories on legal documents or, with scant exception, offer valid testimony in court. This sweeping exclusion from roles of meaningful public responsibility carries with it a sense of infantilization that is both affirmed and explained in another Talmudic source. Seeking to understand the core feature held in common by women, minors, and slaves that explains their invalidation as witnesses, the anonymous Talmudic editor finds it precisely in their diminished status as people "not included in all the commandments" (BT *Bava Kamma* 88a).

We are brought back again to halakha's insistence upon prohibiting any conceivable conflict that might compromise a woman's role as nurturing servant to her husband and family. This principle is extended outward to encompass women's disqualification from serving not only as witnesses, but as judges (BT *Niddah* 49b). Some medieval commentators grappled with how to reconcile this prohibition with the glaring contradiction embodied by Devorah, one of the Bible's titular "judges" (Judges 4:4). Taking midrashic license, they reshape the image of this powerful matriarch, explaining that she was not technically a "judge," but rather something more akin to a schoolteacher. They change her from a legislator and issuer of verdicts to a nurturing educator.

Moreover, while women are technically permitted to bring cases in court, the Talmudic editor notes approvingly that it is not their custom to do so, glorifying this behavior as the fulfillment of a biblical verse. This verse potently captures the attitude of traditional halakha with respect to the correct relationship between women and the public sphere: "All the honor of a daughter is inside" (Ps. 45:14). Maimonides extends a midrash precluding women from becoming queens into a sweeping ruling prohibiting Jewish communities from appointing women to any position of public service (Heb. *kol mesimot she-b'yisrael*; *Mishneh Torah*, Laws of Kings 1:5).

What emerges from the halakhic structures regulating women's interaction with the public sphere is a picture of a person who has no responsibility to go to court, whose witness is not valid, who cannot judge cases of her peers or serve her community in any collective capacity. Her role is not to evaluate or contribute to the culture in which she lives. She is an onlooker, not a shaper, of her social reality, and this is something to be encouraged and prized.

This halakhic gender-ethos was passionately advanced by Israel's widely revered first Chief Rabbi, Abraham Isaac Kook, in the 1920s to support his ruling that according to halakha Jewish women should be denied the right to vote. Rabbi Kook's 1920 responsum on this matter, analyzed in depth by Tova Hartman,[41] sounds an alarm about the great threat to family harmony women's suffrage would inevitably cause: "Through the tempest of opinions and their divisions, the status of home peace is destroyed."[42] In other words, if wives are allowed to vote, this might move them to form opinions in contradiction to those held by their husbands. In the judgment of the first Chief Rabbi of the State of Israel, family stability cannot bear multiple points of view; therefore, the husband's must rule. Anything that impinges on his absolute whim endangers the marriage. The wife must sacrifice the ability to determine who will rule her life in order to satisfy a vision of the home in which one point of view must dominate. Fundamentally, what underlies the intelligibility of this position is the basic halakhic structure of marriage: he acquires her, and thus his will is the defining feature of the marriage. Once again, "the authority of others" circumscribes key dimensions of her life experience.

The Fate of Women in Orthodoxy

To say that halakha expresses an attitude of male agency/superiority and female passivity/inferiority is not necessarily to say that halakhically observant women experience their lives under a dark veil of oppression. The negotiation with the authoritative religious framework is ultimately an individual matter, and the ways in which tradition is psychologically appropriated as a lived experience differ from one religiously observant person to the next. As Tova Hartman has shown with respect to the *niddah/mikveh* rituals, Orthodox Jewish women are far from homogeneous in their attitudes toward and lived practices of aspects of halakha that they find offensive to their sense of personal autonomy. Those living happily within the tradition should not be accused of exhibiting "false consciousness."[43] Similarly, married couples may choose to negotiate egalitarian relationships within the broader halakhic system and simply ignore or compartmentalize the gender ethos out of which some of its rules were framed.

When problems like that of the *aguna* arise, however, this rift in the moral bedrock of halakha is exposed. *Why has the halakhic issue of the* aguna *not been solved?* In light of the great creativity that has been exhibited throughout the history of the rabbinic tradition to solve knotty halakhic issues of communal urgency, the failure to relieve the suffering of the *aguna* can only be attributed to a strong force of resistance within the tradition itself. The *aguna* issue has not been solved because, despite the suffering it causes, it has been deemed by many traditional halakhic authorities to safeguard a core value of the Jewish tradition.

At the root of this ideology can be found the image of woman as nurturer: she holds the child, feeds it milk, and sustains its life. That paradigm, of course, caught the imagination of earlier cultures, in which women were also divested of agency in major spheres of their lives. The image of Sara, the matriarch, waiting "in the tent"; the midrash that poignantly narrates how Rebecca, after Sara's passing, steps into her role to provide light and warmth within the home—these "role models" dominate the tradition's perception, and legislation, of women's roles at every stage of their lives. The decisive concern is that women remain unfailingly available to meet the family's needs, a structure that clearly precludes relational egalitarianism. Thus, traditional halakha has largely appropriated for itself an image of God that sees divesting women of agency and autonomy for the sake of "family harmony" as a gift of His benevolence and wisdom toward His Chosen People.

For this reason, I am not optimistic about the future of incremental legal reform to protect women from the halakhic abuse of *aguna* status. While I support those who endeavor to do so and hope their work is helpful to women imprisoned in marriage, in my view this approach fails to recognize or address the depth of the tradition's insistence that women occupy a secondary, diminished status with respect to men. Notwithstanding good-faith attempts to employ existing halakhic principles to solve the *aguna* issue internally, the wife's status remains essentially as an object of property to the husband, totally subservient to his will. Prohibited from autonomously defining certain key aspects of her experience, she lacks control over her destiny and future. *Reshut acherim aleha*: she lives always in the shadow of another's authority. Whatever exhortations can be found within traditional sources about how a husband should treat his wife, these do nothing to alter the fundamental relational inequality. There is still a master-servant dynamic embedded at the deepest levels of marriage and divorce law. It is for this reason, in my opinion, that the tradition has proved so resistant to altering these laws in any way, despite the widespread suffering they cause and in the face of increasing communal pressure. For many

Orthodox traditionalists, it is in these very laws that a central tenet of halakhic ideology has been preserved.

In critiquing this ideology, modern liberalism and feminism reflect a deep understanding of what it means to be created in the image of God. Egalitarianism can be seen as a meaningful advance in our application of one of the biblical Creation narrative's central themes: that the God of Creation does not encode ontological distinctions between man and woman; that power is not given to one to abuse the other. The moral intuition that moves us to appropriate this image of God as constitutive of our religious vision should absolutely be embraced by and integrated into the halakhic system. If our moral sensibility bridles at the gender imbalance found within the ideology and structure of traditional halakha, we must allow our own, ongoing halakhic process to be mediated by an alternate image of the Divine, with corresponding adjustments in the types of gender policies seen as manifesting God's wisdom and will. If we see in the figure of the "nurturing servant" or "pleasant instrument" not a timeless beneficence founded on God's objective knowledge, but the systemic subjugation of one social group by another mediated by historical mores, we must allow the divine imagery we appropriate to express that sensibility to shape, in turn, how halakha evolves.

For example, what would it mean to take seriously the theological implications of this verse encapsulating the ethos of the God of Creation—"The Lord is good to all, and His mercy is upon all His works" (Ps. 145:9)—as applied to the halakhic structures of marriage and divorce? If our halakhic process is driven by a quest for God-consciousness, we are led to the conclusion that to experience the God of Creation deeply in our lives is to create normative egalitarian structures that do not justify social hierarchy or abuse, but seek to eradicate it at every opportunity. From this biblical imagery of the universally good and compassionate God emanates a call for halakha to liberate people from the shackles of authoritarian relationships. To the extent that these are allowed to flourish and fester within the halakhic system, its practitioners have failed to comprehend the radical demands implied by this verse in the way that, for example, Rabbi Akiva did:

"Beloved is man, created in God's image" (*Pirkei Avot* 3:18). This shared human status as God's beloved must be the measure halakha strives to meet, and the suffering of those it has traditionally disenfranchised will remain a permanent possibility as long as we fail to structure it according to that deep theological demand.

The rejection of halakhic gender-imbalance thus gives normative expression to the theological appropriation of the God of Creation—allowing this image of God a corrective role in halakha's structuring of human relationships. While this position is not predicated upon the authority of any precedent (see chapter 2), Maimonides appears to follow a similar interpretive procedure when elaborating the laws pertaining to non-Jews. While acknowledging that Jews are not obligated to extend to non-Jews certain social graces deemed overly intimate, he then proceeds to correct the possible inference that their well-being can be generally ignored or neglected:

> Even non-Jews, the Sages commanded to visit their sick, and to bury their dead with the dead of Israel, and to sustain their impoverished among the impoverished of Israel, because of the "ways of peace": such that it is written, "*God is good to all, and God's compassion is upon every one of God's creatures*" (Ps. 145:9); as well as, "Its ways are pleasant ways, and all its paths are peace" (Prov. 3:8). [emphasis added][44]

According to Maimonides, the "otherness" that would normally cancel our sense of obligation toward certain others is neutralized or overridden by the principle of the good and compassionate God. Using the same method to a similarly transformative effect, he again appropriates the overriding value expressed by the God of Creation to correct a halakha that seems to leave wide open the possibility of Jewish masters abusing their non-Jewish slaves:

> It is halakhically permissible to overwork non-Jewish slaves. But even though this is the law, decency of character and human understanding dictate that a person should be compassionate

and pursue justice, and should not make the yoke too heavy on his slave and not torment him, and should feed him and give him to drink from all his own [i.e., the master's] food and drink. The Early Sages would give to their servants from every dish that they themselves would eat, and precede the food of the animals and the servants before their own meals.... And similarly one should not humiliate his slave, neither by hand nor with words: for the Torah has consigned him to servitude, not to humiliation. And one should minimize shouting and anger, and instead speak with him pleasantly, and listen to his complaints. Similarly, *among the attributes of God, that God commanded us to emulate, it is written, "... and God's compassion is upon every one of God's creatures"* (Ps. 145:9). And everyone who demonstrates compassion receives it. [emphasis added][45]

While our first response to the above may be to wish Maimonides had used the imagery of the good and compassionate God to justify the abolition of slavery from halakha altogether, the use to which he does put this interpretive method—radical transformation of the institution of slavery as halakhically conceived—is nonetheless quite striking. It is in the hands of anyone prepared to engage meaningfully with the halakhic system to extend the scope of what we understand this principle to cover. It is tempting to imagine what halakhic consciousness and practice might look like if they were permeated by the theme of Creation. Modern liberalism and contemporary feminism have given us an opportunity to experience this spirit. Its integration within the halakhic system should be seen not as a threat or a move toward secularization, but as an unfolding of the normative implications of a compassionate Creator.

Can the halakhic community begin to organize itself around a different set of theological motifs? The hermeneutic of seeking to honor the intrinsic dignity of each human life, implied by the God of Creation, has not been fully actualized within the halakha as it has developed to its current state. But there is a radical possibility to appropriate this principle in the way we build communal life. Applying a halakhic hermeneutic of God-consciousness that appropriates as its guiding spirit the good and compassionate God would undoubtedly lead to fundamental reinterpretations of the sources underpinning marriage and divorce law and to an evolution of halakha itself. Such an approach would obviously meet resistance (perhaps an understatement) from the many traditionalist-halakhic communities that have elevated fear of change to the status of a central religious value. In the following chapters I will explain this overarching rejectionist attitude regarding halakhic evolution as itself both resulting from and supported by a particular image of God: the meta-halakhic God of Stasis. The challenge for individuals and communities at various stages of halakhic exploration and commitment is to decide which set of divine imagery is most authentic to their own moral sensibilities and should thus be appropriated as the guiding spirit of their own halakhic lives.

4

BIOLOGY OR COVENANT?

Conversion and the Corrupting Influence of Gentile Seed

As a young congregational rabbi, I was so given over to the task of educating my congregants about the positive aspects of Jewish observance that many of halakha's darker moral trends remained hidden to me. My awakening to the moral issues of halakha did not happen overnight, but as an evolving process often sparked initially by a series of memorable interactions with sincere, searching Jews who approached me seeking solutions to wrenching dilemmas that my rigorous halakhic training had not prepared me to anticipate.

One of these instances remains especially vivid to me, even some fifty years later. A member of my synagogue in Montreal—a loving person and a serious, intellectual Jew who attended synagogue every Shabbat and was a fixture at my weekly lectures—walked into my office with an irrepressible smile. This was already good news. Forty-five years old, this congregant (we'll call him "Peter") had had trouble falling in love and finding a partner to share his life with. This frustration had worn on Peter over so many years, and I couldn't recall ever having seen him so full of joy as he appeared that day in my study.

The explanation was not long in coming. "Rabbi," he said, "I have found the dream of my life." He had met someone with whom, for the first time, he felt the spark of love that eluded him for so long. As it turned out, I knew the woman: "Susan" was another congregant who regularly attended my services and lectures, and I knew her to be, like Peter, a dedicated and interested Jew. Peter's renewed sense of optimism at finding love had invigorated him, and his vitality was contagious. He wanted to know if I would be the rabbi to marry them; he did not want to wait any longer than necessary. I said of course I would be happy to officiate and asked him to come back the next day with his future bride to have a pre-marriage discussion and explore possible dates.

The next day, Peter arrived alone. He seemed an entirely different person than the one I had seen the day before. With a sad expression and an utterly downtrodden manner, he told me that he had just experienced the most tragic moment of his life. Having shared the fulfillment of his life's dream with an Orthodox Jewish friend, he had met with a rude awakening. The friend responded by explaining to Peter that halakha prohibited him from marrying the woman with whom he had fallen so deeply in love. As it turned out, Susan had not been born a Jew, but had voluntarily chosen a Jewish identity through conversion. Peter was a *kohen*, a descendant of the Jewish priestly class responsible for implementing the sacrificial rites when the Temples stood in Jerusalem. Those whose family traditions designate as bearers of this priestly identity still maintain certain prohibitions and privileges under halakha. For example, a tradition that remains active under Orthodox halakha prohibits *kohanim* from marrying converts (as well as divorcees). While not fully observant by Orthodox standards, Peter took tradition seriously, and so he took this news seriously. I could see with my own eyes that it had shaken him to the core.

"I am disqualified from marrying her," he said, dazed. His whole being seemed to buckle under the weight of this unbearable, inscrutable decree. He was not even looking to me, I felt, for guidance; it was as if he had already given up hope.

Before sharing how I responded to Peter's dilemma in my study all those years ago, I would like to take some time to outline and discuss the process by which one might approach such a weighty halakhic decision. This will provide us with another opportunity to elaborate upon the type of interpretive process I have described as being guided by a hermeneutic of God-consciousness. Let us now investigate the halakhic basis for the disqualification of male *kohanim* from marrying female converts.

An Unresolved Conceptual Tension

Within Jewish tradition, one of the ways in which *kohanim* are set apart from the rest of the Jewish people is by being subject to stricter standards of spiritual purity/impurity (Heb. *tahara/tum'a*). For example, halakha prohibits priests from entering cemeteries because of the proximity to dead bodies—according to tradition, the very paradigm of spiritual impurity. The prohibition from marrying converts is a variation on this theme, for female converts are automatically categorized by halakha under the label "promiscuous" (Heb. *zona*; Maimonides, *Mishneh Torah*, Laws of Forbidden Relations 18:1). Sexual promiscuity, of course, carries its own deep resonance of spiritual impurity for the religious imagination and thus requires special distancing measures for the maintenance of priestly purity.

The automatic designation of female converts as promiscuous begs larger questions about halakha's understanding of converts' status. The tradition, as we shall see, is full of contradictions and tensions on this question and does not offer a univocal response. The tensions seem to revolve around the meaning of conversion itself, and consequently the role the convert plays within the Jewish community post-conversion. Are converts considered unqualified members of the Jewish people, with the dignities and entitlements full status implies, or are there ways in which their past never really leaves them? Will they always have an imperfect or incomplete identity as Jews?

In fact, searching within the tradition we find an unresolved conceptual tension in the convert's status: between identity drawn from choice and behavior, and identity as a biological gift of the God of Israel. Which of these is constitutive of the covenantal relationship with God? If converts are to be seen as full members of the Jewish people, it must be the former, as by definition they lack the latter. And yet we find a powerful strain within halakhic thinking indicating that the power of Jewish identity is a result of being conceived very literally by a man transmitting sperm into a Jewish woman's egg to form a Jewish embryo. For these sources, conception and birth within a Jewish framework are the most significant factors in a person's Jewish identity status. Without it, covenantal commitment to a religious Jewish lifestyle constitutes a meaningful, but ultimately secondary, dimension of a person's status within the Jewish community.

Transcendence through Spiritual Rebirth

There are many traditional sources that seem to assign to converts full status as Jews. In Maimonides's codification of the conversion procedure, once sincere intention is established, the convert is swiftly embraced into the fold of the Jewish community:

> How are religious converts received? When a person comes to convert, and is investigated and no ulterior motives are found, say to him or her: "Why do you want to convert? Don't you know that the Jewish people, in these times, are distressed and persecuted and oppressed and harried and afflicted." If the person says, "I know, and I am prepared"—*receive him or her immediately.*[emphasis added][1]

This passage, with its simple standards and low-key tone, conveys a generally easy, positive attitude toward the reception of converts. This openness appears to continue into the characterization of the status of the new convert. When Maimonides states, "A convert, upon conversion, is like a newborn baby,"[2] he seems to be describing nothing less than a complete erasure of the previous identity with a concurrent total embrace of the new one. Indeed, halakha takes the notion of rebirth to a literal extreme, ruling that all incest taboos toward the convert's biological family are, upon conversion, lifted. Were the male convert's mother or sister to follow his lead and convert to Judaism, he would, according to Maimonides, be free to marry them. Whether or not these cases were ever actualized, their attitude toward the convert's status—erasure of the old identity for the new one—seems clearly conveyed.

We should perhaps not be surprised to find a positive attitude toward conversion within the tradition of the Talmud, which elsewhere places a strong value on personal spiritual achievement over and above spiritual gifts received through hereditary means. A mishnah ranks different classes of people according to who should be prioritized by the community to rescue from danger. First, it runs through the list of hereditary classes, in order of greatest to least priority—or, as it were, best to worst seed. "The *kohen* takes precedence over the Levi; Levi over Israel [i.e., the general population]; Israel over the bastard...." Then it adds a qualification that transforms the entire value-pole of the discussion. "When is this? When they are all equal. But if there were a bastard–Torah scholar, and a *kohen*-ignoramus, the bastard–Torah scholar takes precedence over the *kohen*-ignoramus" (*Mishnah Horayot* 3:8).

This mishnah juxtaposes two paradigms: the high priest who performs the sacred rites, and the bastard who has transformed his life. The bastard has bad seed: the biological pedigree is fraught with sin and corruption. The high priest is a descendent of Aaron, carrier of the most sacred sperm. Which of these takes precedence as the ground of identity: identity born from sacred sperm, or identity born form learning and personal achievement? The mishnah states clearly that the self-created bastard–Torah scholar takes precedence over the biologically superior high priest–ignoramus. In doing so, it brings this important cultural dichotomy into sharp relief, indicating its preference for personal achievement.

In other words, while the hereditary rankings are still maintained relative to each other, a new value has been introduced with the power to transcend them categorically. That power is derived from the personal achievement of Torah study, through which the stigma of one's hereditary identity is effectively erased. Perhaps the spirit embracing the bastard who has achieved greatness in a life devoted to Torah study is the same spirit that embraces converts who voluntarily dedicate themselves to a life of Jewish spiritual discipline. Covenantal identity has the power completely to transform and supplant all that came before.

It is clarifying to consider the image of God underlying this notion of covenantal identity. The God of the covenant prizes covenantal fidelity to such an extent that what seems an almost magical gift is offered in return for it: the transcendence of biological ties through total spiritual rebirth, both heralded poetically in the Talmud and literalized by halakha through the removal of incest taboos.

Ovadiah's Question: A Test Case in the Meaning of Jewish Lineage

The attitude toward conversion and converts found within these sources seems to stand in stark contrast to halakha's exclusion of the female convert from eligibility to marry a *kohen*. The exclusion, as mentioned above, is based on the categorization of the female convert as "promiscuous." This designation is based in turn on a presumption about the life she lived before her conversion, among a non-Jewish community assumed to have looser standards of sexual purity. Let us bracket for the moment questions about the legitimacy of making such assumptions in the first place. Based on the sources we have seen thus far, it seems legitimate to ask why we give any halakhic consideration to that pre-Jewish identity in the first place. Haven't we established that all remnants of that past identity are supplanted by the new, covenantal one? We have already seen a powerful halakha that effectively nullifies the convert's previous sexual identity vis-à-vis his or her biological family. Why does the same thinking not apply to the female convert's sexual history, whatever it may have been?

Maimonides, in one of his most important writings, addresses directly the issue of the convert's identity status in terms of his or her past and present communities. He writes that he has received a halakhic question from a proselyte, Ovadiah, known for his wisdom and learnedness. Ovadiah wants to know if, given his non-Jewish background, he is required to make any changes in the fixed liturgical passages affirming one's connection to the historical Jewish people.

> You ask me if you, too, are allowed to say in the blessings and prayers you offer alone or in the congregation: "*Our God*," and

"God of *our* fathers," "You who have sanctified *us* through your commandments," "You who have separated *us*," "You who have chosen *us*," "You who have inherited *us*," "You who have brought *us* out of the Land of Egypt," "You who have worked miracles to *our* fathers," and more of this kind.[3]

In Ovadiah's question, Maimonides has found an ideal test case with which to address publicly the question of the convert's ultimate status upon conversion. But before examining Maimonides's response, we should appreciate that as interesting as the question itself is the fact that it was asked in the first place. Clearly, a situation arose in which Ovadiah's community was resistant to allowing him, a convert, to lead them in public prayer. Why? Because many of the prayers speak explicitly from the perspective of one whose lineage goes back to Abraham, Isaac, and Jacob; from one whose ancestors suffered as slaves in Egypt. Converts, while covenantal partners, cannot claim that family lineage. Because of this "outsider" dimension of his identity, the male convert cannot serve as a legitimate representative of the community in prayer. This, at least, seems to be the premise underlying Ovadiah's question: a sense that in some way, despite his conversion, there is a constitutive element of Jewish identity that he lacks.

This suggestion is not without basis within halakhic tradition. In fact, Ovadiah's question strongly echoes one addressed by the rabbis of the Mishnah centuries earlier. Their subject is the yearly *bikkurim* (first fruits) ceremony conducted when the Temple stood. As part of the Shavuot pilgrimage festival, Jewish farmers throughout Palestine would converge upon Jerusalem bearing the first-ripening fruits of their harvest derived from seven species specified in the Torah to symbolize the agricultural bounty of the Promised Land. At the Temple, each farmer-pilgrim would present his offering to a priest, then make a declaration widely known for its partial inclusion in the Passover Haggadah:

"I acknowledge this day before the Lord your God that I have entered the land that the Lord swore to our fathers to assign us.... My father was a fugitive Aramean. He went down to

Egypt with meager numbers and sojourned there; but there he became a great and very populous nation. The Egyptians dealt harshly with us and oppressed us; they imposed heavy labor upon us. We cried to the Lord, the God of our fathers, and the Lord heard our plea and saw our plight, our misery, and our oppression. The Lord freed us from Egypt by a mighty hand, by an outstretched arm and awesome power, and by signs and portents. He brought us to this place and gave us this land, a land flowing with milk and honey.... Look down from Your holy abode, from heaven, and bless Your people Israel and the soil You have given us, a land flowing with milk and honey, as You swore to our fathers."

(Deut. 26:3–15)

This declaration, instituted as an important public affirmation of identity and membership, takes the form of a capsule-history of Jewish peoplehood. The strong emphasis is clearly upon biological lineage. And what of those members of the community who do not share in this lineage? This is the question taken up by the Mishnah:

These are the ones who bring [i.e., the first-fruits offering] but do not read [i.e., the declaration]: *The convert brings but does not read, for he is unable to say, "... [the land] that God swore to our forefathers, and to us"* (Deut. 26:3). If his mother is Jewish, he brings and reads. And when he prays privately, he should say, "... God of the Fathers of Israel"; and when he prays in a synagogue, he should say, "... God of your fathers." And if his mother was Jewish, he should say, "God of our fathers."

(*Mishnah Bikkurim* 1:4; emphasis added)

According to this mishnah, there is indeed an element of Jewish identity that, for converts, is lacking—the connection to historical Jewish peoplehood. This notion of historical identity is conceived of in literal, biological terms. The convert, not sharing in this biological-historical identity, may not read a declaration asserting that he does, for according to this line of thinking, it would simply constitute a false declaration.

There are other traditional sources that extend this sense of a partial or incomplete identity for converts. The mishnah subsequent to the one just discussed takes the convert's exclusion from the *bikkurim* ceremony as a jumping-off point to discuss another halakhic area in which she is set apart from other members of the community, pointedly emphasizing her partial Jewishness. Invoking the biblical prohibition of *kohanim* from marrying female converts, the rabbis of the Mishnah extend the prohibition to include even the *daughter* of converts:

> Rabbi Eliezer ben Yakov says: A woman who is the daughter of converts may not marry a *kohen*—until the mother is Jewish [lit. "from/of Israel"].... Even until ten generations, until the mother is Jewish.
>
> (*MISHNAH BIKKURIM* 1:5)

The principle, repeated for emphasis, is that a complete Jewish identity is one that is distanced not only behaviorally, but biologically, from any connection to a non-Jewish past. Even if a person chooses to abandon his or her former lifestyle completely and join the Jewish covenantal community, there is still some element of that past that sticks, equated in the Rabbinic imagination with spiritual impurity and thus a threat to the spiritual integrity of the Jewish people. "Until his mother is from Israel" clearly announces the understanding that conception with Jewish seed and/or birth from a Jewish womb ("holy conception" and "holy birth," respectively; see *Mishneh Torah*, Laws of First-Fruit Offerings 11:13) transmits levels of holiness and status within the community. Conception mediates holiness and bestows ontological status, missing from those not conceived or born within the biological framework of the Jewish tradition.

It is thus the primacy of the biological identity and the anxiety caused by its absence that motivates this halakhic voice seeking to maintain converts' pre-Jewish status (and stigma) as part of their Jewish identity and regulate their behavior even after they have become covenantal members of the Jewish people. This perspective is clearly in tension with the strain of Rabbinic thinking discussed above, which invests covenantal commitment with the power of total spiritual rebirth. What we have then, again, is conflicting paths of halakhic decision making guided by divergent images of God: the covenantal God, we might say, versus the biological God; a God whose power and experience are mediated exclusively by religious behavior versus mediated by a notion of "holy seed."

The "Holy Seed"

Historians of halakha trace the power of the "holy seed" tradition back to the biblical book of Ezra, which credits its titular character with leading the religious revival of the Jewish people returning to Palestine after the destruction of the First Temple and subsequent Babylonian Exile (c. 586–536 BCE). Many Jews returned with foreign wives acquired from the local populations among whom they had settled. Prior to Ezra's time, conversion was seen as more of a national than a religious phenomenon, a word describing social integration into the Jewish people by way of national conquest or, in fact, marriage. The convert (Heb. *ger*) was the one who came to live (Heb. *lagur*) among the Jews. The religious dimension of this lifestyle was seen to be implied, and perhaps therefore is given less prominent emphasis than the social, in an era of human history that did not necessarily see these as two separate spheres. We find this hierarchy within the well-known announcement of the most famous biblical convert, Ruth, who first proclaims to her Jewish mother-in-law, "Your people shall be my people," only then following, "and Your God my God" (Ruth 1:16). In this early biblical construction of conversion, with the Jewish people firmly ensconced in their ancient homeland, connection to Jewish peoplehood was seen automatically to lead to Jewish faith.[4]

Ezra, challenged to rebuild a Jewish community with a weakened sense of political sovereignty in their land, shifted the emphasis of conversion from social integration to religious commitment. He feared the threat of religious syncretism posed by tens of thousands of idolatrous spouses and, pivotally, framed this threat in biological terms, establishing "holy seed"—that is, conception by biologically Jewish parents—as a dominant criterion of Jewish identity (Ezra 9–10; Nehemiah 9:2; 10:31; 13:1–8; 13:23–28). Thus, in a stark departure from previous policy, he ruled that the Jewish men returning from exile must separate themselves entirely from the wives and children they brought back with them. Without nullifying conversion in principle, he transformed its meaning significantly, emphasizing biological purity as a stave against the looming threat posed by the polluting backgrounds of those seeking Jewish membership.

In the Rabbinic period, the principle of purely religious conversion was introduced: formal procedures for entering into the community of Israel defined by shared normative belief structures. Here the covenantal notion of conversion became more strongly emphasized. The proper intention, coupled with the proper procedure—a commitment to mitzvah observance, a ritual immersion, standing before a Jewish court—could facilitate the type of spiritual rebirth discussed above. The term "brother in mitzvot" enters the Talmudic lexicon to ascribe limited familial status to non-Jewish slaves and converts: those whose roots lie outside of the Jewish gene pool, but who are bound together by shared normative and theological commitments.

At the same time, as we have seen, the tradition that preserves the "strangeness" of the convert receives ongoing halakhic expression as well. Ezra's "holy seed" finds inverse expression in the Talmud's characterization of non-Jewish sperm as a "tainted drop." It is the negative valence attributed to this genetic transmission of identity that motivates the Rabbis to invalidate not only female converts from marrying *kohanim*, as prescribed in the Torah, but their offspring as well (BT *Kiddushin* 78a; see also *Mishnah Yadayim* 4:4 on the "stickiness" of ethnic identity both post-conversion and in considerations of whether to allow conversion to certain ethnic groups).

Moreover, particularly in the medieval period, this tradition of biological spirituality—a strong motif of Jewish mysticism—was bolstered by the writings of popular kabbalists, foremost among them perhaps Rabbi Yehuda Halevi of Spain. According to Halevi, the transcendent power of *kedusha* (sanctity) is built into the Jewish soul at its creation. Jewish identity is, at its essence, not a personal achievement but a genetic one.[5]

A Theological-Halakhic Crossroads

This, in effect, is the theological-halakhic crossroads at which Maimonides found himself upon receiving Ovadiah's query. The question of whether Ovadiah could pray using the first-person possessive with respect to Jewish history ("God of *our* fathers"; "You who have chosen *us*"; "You who have brought *us* out of the Land of Egypt") is ultimately a question of status: to what extent have converts achieved ontological parity with their fellow Jews? To what extent can religious faith overcome the borders of family identity: biological lineage, shared experiences of suffering and joy? Can converts overcome the barriers of lived history and feel they participate fully through an empathic identification with Jewish history and memory?

Maimonides's legal ruling to Ovadiah is less significant than the prominence to which he gives the question by answering it in such a theologically substantive, passionate, and public way. The ruling itself he dispatches with immediately—"Yes, you may say all this in the prescribed order and not change it in the least"—before proceeding with the substance of what he wants to teach:

> The reason for this is, that Abraham our Father taught the people, opened their minds, and revealed to them the true faith and the unity of God; he rejected the idols and abolished their adoration; he brought many children under the wings of the Divine Presence; he gave them counsel and advice, and ordered his sons and the members of his household after him to keep the ways of the Lord forever, as it is written, "For I have known him to the end that he may command his children, and his household after him, that he may keep the ways of the Lord, to do righteousness and justice" (Gen. 18:19). Ever since then whoever adopts Judaism and confesses the unity of the Divine Name, as it is prescribed in the Torah, is counted among the

disciples of Abraham our Father, peace be with him. These men are Abraham's household, and he it is who converted them to righteousness.

In the same way as he converted his contemporaries through words and teaching, he converts future generations through the testament he left to his children and household after him. Thus Abraham our Father, peace be with him, is the father of his pious posterity who keep his ways, *and the father of his disciples and of all proselytes who adopt Judaism.* [emphasis added][6]

For Maimonides, the constitutive principle of Jewish identity is not biology but covenantal behavior, as encapsulated in the words of God to Abraham: "… that he may … keep the way of the Lord by doing what is just and right" (Gen. 18:19). Maimonides holds the covenantal principle as a transforming framework for the barriers of ethnicity and family experience. Being called upon to live a certain way of life breaks through all ethnic borders, forging a connection with the Jewish forefather Abraham that is, he suggests, far more significant than any notion of "holy seed." The only meaningful standard for becoming "disciples of Abraham" is the adoption of a Jewish lifestyle and confession of divine unity.

Maimonides is almost mischievous, and certainly pointed, in the mixture of metaphors he uses to bring his point home: converts are every bit as much members of "Abraham's household" as his biological descendents; future generations of Jews are every bit as much "converts" as converts themselves ("he converts future generations through the testament he left to his children and household after him"). Abraham, again, is equally "the father of his disciples and of all proselytes who adopt Judaism." Thus converts, as capable of meeting covenantal standards as any other Jew, can and should say the prayers as they are written, claiming the fullness of Jewish history, memory, and identity as their own.

Maimonides repeats this point in several different ways, with several different emphases, seeming intent on foreclosing any possibility of misunderstanding or misuse of his words.

There is no difference whatever between you and us. You shall certainly say the blessing, "Who has chosen us," "Who has given
us," "Who have taken us for Your own," and "Who have separated us": for the Creator, may He be extolled, has indeed chosen you and separated you from the nations and given you the
Torah.... Know that our fathers, when they came out of Egypt,
were mostly idolators; they had mingled with the pagans of
Egypt, and imitated their way of life, until the Holy One,
blessed be He, sent Moses our Teacher, the master of all
prophets, who separated us from the nations and brought us all
under the wings of the Divine Presence, us and all proselytes,
and gave to all of us one Law.

Do not consider your origin as inferior. While we are the
descendents of Abraham, Isaac, and Jacob, *you derive from Him
through whose word the world was created.* [emphasis added][7]

It should be noted that this theological discourse was not necessary in
order for Maimonides to give Ovadiah a permissive ruling. While theologically radical, halakhically his opinion is not without precedent: "It
was taught in the name of Rabbi Yehuda: the convert himself both
brings the offering and makes the declaration." In fact, one might see
it as a kind of expanded homily based on the evocative explanation
given by that precedent for the convert's ability to make the *bikkurim*
declaration: "Because Abraham was the father of the entire world" (PT
Bikkurim 1:4).

Clearly, then, Maimonides was not simply interested in resolving
a halakhic question. Were that the case, the answer would have been
much shorter. Maimonides, it seems, was interested in answering the
much larger, perhaps implied question of how one truly and fully
enters the Jewish people; of the nature of Jewish identity. He wanted to
advance the claim that the transforming feature of Jewish identity is
not lineage but faith commitment and the acceptance of divine unity
and a particular way of life. Abraham is not the "father of the world"
via the transmission of his holy seed, but rather via his worldview, his
commitment to the monotheistic principle. He transmits sanctity not

through sperm but through a disciplined faith posture. The significance of the biological is severely circumscribed; the organizing framework of identity is the covenantal relationship, period.

Tellingly, while Maimonides did have halakhic precedent upon which to base his answer to Ovadiah, he does not quote or even mention it. Rather, he ties his halakhic decision to a powerful invocation of a particular image of God: "Do not consider your origin as inferior. While we are the descendents of Abraham, Isaac, and Jacob, you derive from Him through whose word the world was created." It is in this image, of a God who desires relationship mediated by covenantal acceptance—for whom this tie is so powerful that of itself it substitutes, or better constitutes, the most exalted form of lineage—that Maimonides chooses to ground his halakhic response.

Personal versus Public Role

Maimonides's letter to Ovadiah gives us a clear picture of his theological conception of conversion, as well as a strong model of halakhic decision making that foregrounds theological concerns. In his comprehensive halakhic opus, the *Mishneh Torah*, when Maimonides arrives at the halakhic issue of the convert's role in the *bikkurim* ceremony,[8] his ruling there is consistent: converts can indeed both offer sacrifices and make the declaration affirming their connection to Jewish history and peoplehood. Moreover, he gives the reason there supplied by the Talmudic precedent, complete with a poetic embellishment that invokes and perhaps even alludes to the spirit of his words to Ovadiah:

> For as God says to Abraham, "I have made you the father of many nations" (Gen. 17:5). We see, then, that he is the father of the entire world [of people] who enter under the wings of His presence [Heb. *Shekhina*].[9]

Maimonides's letter, however, did not silence other strains within the tradition privileging biological sanctity and identity. In fact, he records many of them himself in the *Mishneh Torah*. These rulings seem to stand in stark contrast to his theological position regarding converts and liturgy articulated in the letter.

> It is prohibited to establish a king from the community of converts, even after several generations—until his mother is Jewish [lit. "from Israel"]. As it is written, "And you may not appoint upon yourselves a gentile man, *for he is not your brother*" (Deut. 17:15). And this applies not only to kingship, but to any position of Jewish communal service—not to any military position, or even to be the person in charge of supervising irrigation to the fields. It goes without saying that a judge or a prince may only be one who is biologically Jewish [lit. "from Israel"]. As it says, "From among your brothers, appoint yourself a king" (ibid.)—all positions of authority that you appoint upon yourselves should only come from "among your brothers." [emphasis added][10]

In Maimonides's letter, the choice to embrace the God of Abraham imbues the convert with a powerful pedigree that trumps biological lineage. Yet here in the *Mishneh Torah*, we find it stated plainly, and repeatedly, that the convert is not considered "your brother." This is a family term; the convert can never fully be a brother because he does not share the spiritual biology of a Jew, lacking the holy seed, the holy womb: "until his mother is Jewish."

The other expression in dealing with the convert's public role within the Jewish people is that he is not "from among the *choice ones* [Heb. *me-muvkhar*] among your brothers" (BT *Bava Kamma* 88a). According to this line of thinking, to whatever extent they may find membership within the "brotherhood of mitzvot," converts, like non-Jewish slaves, will always maintain a second-class stigma. They are not "choice ones" among their chosen community. Their biology has been spiritually corrupted in a way that can never fully be rectified. Having come themselves from the "tainted drop" of their parents' sexual union, their own inescapable makeup carries that taint within themselves and passes it on to their children "until his mother is from Israel."

A Deeply Rooted Tension

There are several other instances in which Maimonides, in his role as halakhist, encodes Talmudic precedents that seem starkly at odds with the vision of conversion he offers in his letter to Ovadiah. This is not an uncommon occurrence in the study of Maimonides, and scholars have argued for centuries about the relationship between his theological and halakhic writings. Here we find a particularly stark illustration of one such contradiction. How could the same person who insisted that the pedigree of the convert comes directly from God and therefore must in no way be considered inferior to that of biological Jews, explicitly rule elsewhere that the convert is, in fact, inferior? Why does this powerful theological principle disappear from a halakha that bans the convert from public office? Given that he has committed himself to the covenantal God of the Jewish people, what holds the tradition back from full acceptance as "your brother"? Maimonides's theology here seems absent as a factor shaping halakhic practice, which is determined instead by a more hard-and-fast figuration of biology and ethnicity.

We need not attempt neatly to resolve this contradiction, which as we now can see reflects a tension deeply rooted within not only Rabbinic but biblical tradition. Maimonides demonstrates that this tension remains quite alive and, in his attempt to negotiate it, raises a rich set of questions of its own. To what degree does our religious understanding of God enter into our religious practice? Is the codification of Jewish legal precedent the exclusive factor binding halakhic Jews, or is there a deeper religious moment in our connection to God that may shape, guide, and correct halakhic observance?

In the letter to Ovadiah, Maimonides passionately and poetically emphasizes that covenantal choice and commitment are the most powerful constitutive features of Jewish identity and discounts biological spirituality as secondary. Identity is defined by faith and practice. The intention of the letter seems clearly to lead the Jewish community forward in this direction, to open these new possibilities for thinking about religious priorities, our conception of God, and how these might impact our notions of membership. He is intent on stressing the importance of allowing the theological, experiential impulse of the service of God to act as a corrective to the codification of the law.

Elsewhere, in his halakhic writing, we find that codification of the law remains intact irrespective of his religious vision—perhaps due to the weight of established precedent, which he did not feel he had the authority to overturn; perhaps because he felt it was impossible or unwise to legislate against communal attitudes and knew the Jewish community of his time was not prepared to accept a sweeping new set of halakhic innovations around conversion. Where he could find a precedent, as in the case of the *bikkurim* declaration, he used it. Otherwise he let the law stand as it was.

As contemporary Jews grappling with our own halakhic dilemmas, are we bound to follow Maimonides's precedent in this regard? Must we be willing to suspend our theological intuitions and moral conscience, to observe and perpetuate forms of behavior with which we feel deeply, personally at odds? I would argue that we may allow ourselves to be inspired by the halakhic hermeneutic of God-consciousness modeled by Maimonides in his letter to Ovadiah without adopting his stance with regard to limitations of precedent. We find within halakhic history divergent attitudes toward conversion based upon distinct theological conceptions of God, covenant, and the nature of the soul. The choice of which of these attitudes to emphasize as we create our own halakhic history is in our hands.

A Clear Moral Intuition

We should now have a fuller understanding of the halakhic situation in which Peter, my congregant-*kohen* who despaired after discovering an insurmountable halakhic barrier to marrying the love of his life, found himself that day in my study. The female convert is assigned the halakhic status of a "promiscuous woman" (Heb. *zona*) because of her non-Jewish past. The commitment to live covenantally in this instance does not render her a newborn baby. Her tainted seed remains, and the *kohen* must be protected from it.

I knew Susan, the woman Peter wanted to marry. She was, as I mentioned earlier, an active, interested, searching member of the congregation. According to halakhic tradition, her lack of a Jewish mother rendered her automatically to be categorized as promiscuous. But do we simply dole out denigrating statuses to people irrespective of reality? Do we then allow these incoherent status designations to determine the most important decisions of our lives? The more I thought about it, the more morally problematic it seemed—not only to stamp her with this stigma, but to insist that she and Peter break off their relationship because of it. Ironically, the fact of the matter was that Susan was more modest than many of the "fully" Jewish women in my congregation. Are we bound by a picture of the non-Jewish woman based upon ancient history? Even in light of an alternative theological tradition that sees conversion as covenantal rebirth with the power even to erase blood ties (and taboos) anchoring the convert in his or her biological past?

When Peter approached me with the tragic news that he was going to have to break his engagement, I had not studied the issue of conversion with the thoroughness of the above discussion. My response was immediate, drawn from a clear moral intuition. I felt compelled by this middle-age man who had finally found a woman he loved and wanted to start a family with. Refusing marriage seemed to cause him pain unjustly. Moreover, I could not in good conscience allow the incoherent, morally problematic designation of Susan as promiscuous to permeate the way I thought about her or influence my decision in this most delicate and meaningful moment of her life. The notion of telling these two very serious Jewish seekers that they must deny themselves the happiness of marriage because of this now-obscure, ancient principle seemed unacceptable as the ground for destroying their dream to build a new life. I told Peter that I would be honored to perform the wedding.

Now that the halakhic and theological issues around conversion are even clearer to me, having examined the relevant traditions, I find my initial moral intuition supported. No more now than then am I prepared to live, and insist that others live, according to a mythologized genealogy. I cannot be bound, or insist that others be bound, by a halakhic theology that privileges certain kinds of sperm, wombs, and genes and stigmatizes others, when everything I understand about the root of Judaism points to its essence as a spiritual system grounded in behavioral norms and theological insights open equally to everyone. I did not believe then, nor do I now, that "chosenness" is a result of onto-logical uniqueness. In this I stand firmly with Maimonides's heartening exhortation to Ovadiah: all are potentially the children of Abraham, whom God appointed as the carrier of a covenantal vision for history.

Thus, I cannot speak to any potentially negative spiritual-biological consequences resulting from my decision to encourage Peter and Susan to follow through on their plans to marry or my deci-sion to officiate at their wedding. I can only attest that it was an extremely joyful occasion.

5

WHERE DID MODERN ORTHODOXY GO WRONG?

The Mistaken Halakhic Presumptions of Rabbi Soloveitchik

Rabbi Joseph B. Soloveitchik *zz"l*, my beloved teacher and mentor, would have disagreed in the strongest possible terms with my decision to marry Peter and Susan. He would not have seen it as a joyous occasion, but one of mourning for the loss of something far greater than the love of two people. I can say this confidently because he once described, in a lecture, his response when a parallel case had come before him.

A woman had converted to Judaism out of what Soloveitchik acknowledged approvingly as a pure desire to join the Jewish people. Eventually she met a Jewish boy whose background had given him little exposure to his heritage. Over the course of their relationship, she brought him closer to Jewish tradition. They got engaged. Prior to the wedding, out of the new desire to explore his roots she had kindled, her fiancé visited the cemetery where his grandfather was buried. On the grave, he found symbols indicating that he was a *kohen*, a descendent of the priestly line—whom, we will remember, halakha prohibits from marrying converts.

Soloveitchik expressed keen sympathy with the tragic, bitter irony of this couple's dilemma. Nevertheless, with no hesitation, he told her she must leave and could not marry him.

> With sadness in my heart, and I share in the suffering of the poor
> woman, or the poor girl, who was instrumental in bringing him
> back to the fold, and then she had to lose him. She lost him,
> actually. She walked away. [Transcribed from tape recording]

Soloveitchik concluded his telling of this vignette with a weary sigh:
"All you can say is, I surrender to the will of the Almighty."

From this anecdote emerges a clear theological stance with
respect not merely to the halakha of converts and *kohanim*, but to
halakha in general. In the previous chapter I outlined a different theological-halakhic path leading to a different decision—but it is not
merely that this type of approach would not have occurred to
Soloveitchik or that he would have respected but disagreed with it.
Actually, he would have considered my decision heretical, transgressing basic theological precepts about the God who revealed the Torah
to the Jewish people and the nature of that Torah.

Because of Soloveitchik's stature to modern Orthodox Jews and
especially rabbis, his theology of halakha—which, as I will explain, acts
as a kind of shield keeping the system impervious to the possibility of
what he would have called "external" critique: historical, psychological,
philosophical, and so forth—permeates the ethos of that community far
beyond those with direct exposure to his written and spoken words. In
this chapter, I will describe and analyze some key precepts of this theology, some of its sources in the Talmudic tradition, and the image of
God it both cultivates and is guided by. This explanation takes us out of
an examination of particular halakhic cases or concepts and into the
sphere of "meta-halakha." Before proceeding, it will be useful to explain
what that means and how it can be used to understand the strong tendency within modern Orthodoxy to reject halakhic change.

Love of Perfection, Fear of Change, and the Meta-Halakhic God of Stasis

Depending on where you locate yourself on the spectrum of religious
conservatism/progressivism, the halakhic critiques and suggestions
offered in the previous two chapters may seem revolutionary, modest,

or quaintly outdated. Within much, if not most, of the Orthodox halakhic community, it would almost certainly be considered blasphemy, far outside the pale even of legitimate discussion.

Let us ask the obvious question: why?

The answer does not lie in an analysis of the particulars of any halakhic concept or case, but rather in the "meta-halakhic" sphere: communal assumptions and convictions about the nature and purpose of halakha that set parameters around how it legitimately may be approached, developed, or even discussed. Clearly, the orientation toward these "meta"-questions would play a determinative role in how halakha and halakhic communities evolve; together, they make up the lens through which any particular halakhic issue will be viewed.

> *Is halakhic change possible or impossible? If it is possible, is it something to be encouraged or deterred?*

These are examples of meta-halakhic questions that have played a critical role in the evolution of contemporary halakhic discourse and practice. For in the modern period the Orthodox community, broadly speaking, has coalesced around a conviction that change per se is destructive to the halakhic system, which must be preserved intact to the greatest extent possible. This preservationist imperative is supported by negative stances on other meta-halakhic questions that join into a theology designed to hold the halakhic system as aloof as possible from encounters with potentially transformative ideas.

> *Is it legitimate to consider the historical contexts out of which certain halakhic traditions emerged when evaluating them today and applying them to modern life? May subjective moral intuition, logical argument, or observed social realities serve as valid bases for critiquing inherited halakha?*

The anti-change theology that has guided so much modern halakhic development is given symbolic religious shape by a particular image of God and His relationship to the Jewish people, revelation, and history.

It is a God who first freed an enslaved people from physical bondage, then "liberated" an exiled people from the contingent, chaotic dimensions of existence by giving them a law that allows them to live within an eternal dimension: a system of norms based upon the unchanging wisdom and will of the Creator. The halakha bestowed by this God frees those who practice it from all forms of contingency and arbitrariness, from the laws of nature and history. It creates a world of comforting stability, kept aloft by a self-affirming system of divine rules. Halakha achieves this "perfection" and "permanence," in this view, by refusing to acknowledge that changes in history should affect the halakhic process.

What is traded for this permanence rooted in the denial that historical processes may influence halakhic development?

One thing lost is our subjective experience of reality—reality as we see and know it, as opposed to reality as described by inherited tradition. For in order to participate in what might be called the "revelatory dimension" mediated by halakhic practice, this God of Halakhic Permanence demands the sacrifice of human moral and logical faculties. In exchange for the stability of an eternal dimension removed from history, the needs of the present and concerns of the future always play a secondary, sacrificial role in halakhic consideration. The theology of halakhic perfection is based upon, and thus naturally cultivates, a denial that the vicissitudes of nature and history impinge on the Chosen People, who remain insulated from these trends by virtue of their unflinching grasp on a timeless Tree of Life.

Traditions that come into conflict with emerging moral sensibilities, for example—based perhaps upon exposure to experiences and intellectual currents unavailable to earlier generations—nevertheless stand aloof from possible critique and demand preservation and adherence in the closest possible replication of their inherited forms. Needs and desires that arise out of subjective experience will always be trumped by the objective divine knowledge with which this theology imbues halakhic practice. The system legitimates itself. The knowledge gained by direct observation of human life is disallowed as a relevant factor to critique and guide halakhic development, sacrificed in exchange for participation in a transpersonal sphere of timeless perfection. While this timelessness may resonate with the experience of some, it is prescribed for all—and so subjective experience becomes another sacrificial offering to the meta-halakhic God of Halakhic Infallibility, a God indifferent to history, to the realities of life as it is lived. A God of Stasis.

That this meta-halakhic ideal of perfection, and the rejection of halakhic change it supports and is supported by, has become the prohibitive theology of modern Orthodox Judaism is due largely to the stature of Rabbi Soloveitchik, who articulated it clearly and forcefully at a convention of the Rabbinical Council of America (RCA, the umbrella organization of the American modern Orthodox rabbinate) in 1975. It will be illuminating to examine the context in which he delivered this self-proclaimed manifesto, to consider a cultural crossroads at which the paradigm of ahistorical perfection was challenged and modern halakhic practice might have embarked on a different path.

Emanuel Rackman and the Authenticity of Progress

In chapter 3, examining women's status within halakha, I described the *aguna* problem, women locked into marriages against their will because of the halakhic impossibility of divorcing through their own agency. I mentioned that in the last half-century attempts have been made by a few Orthodox rabbis willing to expose themselves to inevitable and at times ugly public censure, in order to find creative solutions to this halakhic quandary and relieve the suffering of so many women. One of the most famous of these approaches was offered by Rabbi Emanuel Rackman, first at the convention of the RCA mentioned above, and later in his book *Modern Halakha for Our Time*.

Rackman was sympathetic to (he describes himself as "militant and impatient" about) both the personal tragedy of the unsolved *aguna* issue and the problem it posed for halakhic credibility, citing it as a "sore-spot for the status of the Jewish woman—and her justifiable complaints." He felt this festering communal "sore-spot" sent a message to all Jewish women that the system is unable, or unwilling, to respond to the suffering inflicted upon them by this halakhic injustice, much less respond to their evolving self-understanding as equal partners in personal relationships.

The solution Rackman proposed was a form of retroactive marital annulment, based on the model of the "mistaken sale"—monetary transactions annulled for lack of full disclosure by one of the parties. Since in marriage, as in sales, full consent is required by both parties, the withholding of information by one is considered to compromise the other's consent. "Concealing an important fact in selling a piece of property can justify the annulment of the sale. The same argument can be applied with regard to a marriage."[1]

To support this approach, Rackman paraphrased the Talmudic case about a woman whose husband dies and so she finds herself obligated, through ancient levirate practice, to marry one of his surviving brothers, who has leprosy. The Talmud asserts that it should be reasonable to annul the widow's first marriage on the grounds that she never would have consented to marry her husband in the first place with the expectation that she would eventually be obligated to marry her leprous brother-in-law. This logic is accepted, but the Talmud nevertheless disallows the annulment on another ground: the general presumption that women prefer any marriage at all to being alone. Thus, even though this is, technically, a mistaken sale, the alternative—no sale—was understood by the Talmudic Rabbis to be, from the perspective of women themselves, far worse. Thus, they would not be released by annulment even from marriages with men they could not tolerate.

Rackman proposed an appropriation of this logic of annulment, with a critical amendment in its application based on an updated presumption about women's preferences. Outlining his own meta-halakhic approach, he characterized this particular Talmudic presumption, and such presumptions generally, as historically conditioned: "always rebuttable ... never absolute." He acknowledged that the mind-set of preferring a bad marriage to no marriage may have been common among Talmudic women ("The woman who was alone was lost in the society of the times") but concluded simply, "In our day it is no longer true."[2] If this presumption were to be removed and the "mistaken purchase" annulment were to stand, this could prove a halakhic safety net for women with no other recourse to exit their marriages.

> If that presumption is the only thing standing in the way, then it should be possible to annul marriages whenever circumstances develop which she did not anticipate and never would have accepted had she known of them in advance. She ought to be able to say that she married the man, but did not know that he was a sadist; that he was irresponsible; that he would be incompetent; that he would refuse a *get* even for cause.[3]

It is important to note the criteria that seem most strongly at work in Rackman's halakhic decision-making process. For him, the halakhic ruling is guided by the reality of the human situation—the moral and psychological considerations at play, historical and social context— rather than the other way around. He challenges halakha to take into account the reality of the modern woman, who may well prefer being alone to having a miserable marriage with a sadist, an incompetent, or a schlub. In Talmudic times, economic conditions were such that without a man, a woman would be deprived of any support and viewed askew by her community. Is it a meta-halakhic imperative to import and impose those same standards unilaterally upon the contemporary milieu? Must we insist that the same presumption applies to women inherently, across time and culture? Must we insist that women whose subjective experience diverges from this presumption are victims of false-consciousness who have strayed beyond the halakhic pale? May historical context and shifting social conditions enter at all into formulating halakhic principle?

Rackman was open about his embrace of historical context, subjective experience, lived reality, and moral intuition as critical factors in
the evolution of halakha as a vital tradition. In an article published
around the same time as the RCA convention at which he made his
aguna proposal, he published an elaboration of his meta-halakhic
approach, arguing for the acknowledgment and examination of subjective moral priorities as a necessary (if not sufficient) prerequisite of
responsible halakhic decision making:

> Indeed, were more rabbis to be candid, it would be discovered
> that a personal philosophy is a very important factor in the
> process. Needless to say, the conclusion must be based on the
> law, and its vast literature, and the reasoning must be objective
> and able to withstand criticism by peers. The subjective ele-
> ment cannot be the basis for decision, but honesty requires that
> its presence shall not be denied.[4]

He went on to apply this imperative of halakhic subjectivity to an
analysis of why the *aguna* issue had not yet been resolved:

> If rabbis have no sympathy whatever with the demands of
> modern women for equal status in the Jewish law of marriage
> and divorce, they will find texts adequate to support their
> intransigence. If, however, they feel that the present situation is
> simply intolerable and an insult to God and God's law, they will
> be vociferous and militant in making use of the halakhic
> authorities and the texts available to propose revision in the
> halakha.[5]

Rackman emphasized that personal moral inclinations based upon
the evaluation of historical, social, and psychological factors—the
kinds of influences that make up an individual's "personal philosophy"—should not be considered external (and thus invalid) to
the process of halakhic decision making and, moreover, that those
who allow the halakhic process to be guided by it "are not less

'Orthodox' than their colleagues, and, indeed, they may even be more 'authentic.'"[6]

"Any Sort of Husband": Popular Presumptions about Female Preferences

If Rackman chose to make his *aguna* proposal a kind of public test case for his values-based, historically contextualized, reality-affirming approach to halakha, he chose a feature of halakhic tradition that seemed readily amenable to this kind of treatment: *hazaka* (pl. *hazakot*), often translated as "presumption/s." In order to fully understand the significance of Rackman's halakhic stance, as well as Soloveitchik's response to it, it will be helpful to briefly explain this key halakhic concept upon which he builds his case and to add some background to the Talmudic source he quotes.

A *hazaka* is a prediction about nature—in this case, human nature—based on observed patterns of consistency, upon which a halakha or set of halakhot may be based. It is a reasonable expectation about how people generally, and different subsets of people, will respond to different kinds of events: what is likely to be considered advantageous or damaging; what people's preferences are, given different sets of alternatives. It is necessary for legislators to have at least a working model of such presumptions at hand when considering whether a given law will be helpful or harmful and to whom it might be helpful versus harmful. The Rabbis, for example, in the statutes dealing with the giving and receiving of divorce documents, were faced with the issue of how strict or lenient to make the requirements accompanying these procedures. Should it be harder or easier to effectuate a divorce?

For them, this question begged another: do women exhibit a strong, consistent preference to be married versus not married, such that they are willing to make significant sacrifices in the quality of their partner and relationship?

The context of Rackman's Talmudic source concerns the issue of what happens when, subsequent to entering into a binding agreement, unforeseen circumstances evolve that, had they been known, would have prevented one of the parties from entering into the agreement in the first place. "Why," for example, "should a sin offering whose owner died not revert to the state of unconsecration [i.e., returned to the owner, rather than kept for sacrifice by the Temple; a form of monetary reimbursement], for the owner would surely not have set it aside upon such an understanding?" (BT *Bava Kamma* 110b). The Talmud seems to conclude that such agreements should indeed be considered annulled and provides another example to illustrate the principle:

> Why should a deceased brother's wife on becoming bound to one affected with leprosy not be released ... for surely she would not have consented to betroth herself upon this understanding?
>
> (BT *BAVA KAMMA* 110B)

The logic of annulment is accepted here as well. There is only one fact that interferes with its implementation as law: a *hazaka*, a presumption about women's preferences.

> In that case we all can bear witness that she was quite prepared to accept any conditions, as we learn from Resh Lakish; for Resh Lakish said: It is better [for a woman] to dwell as two than to dwell in widowhood.
>
> (BT *BAVA KAMMA* 110B–111A)

In other words, the Talmud seems prepared to accept that if women did indeed prefer living alone to living with a leprous levirate husband, this situation meets the halakhic requirements for annulment. It is the presumption that she prefers a warm body of any kind to no body at all that guides this legislation to a different outcome. Were the presumption to be removed, the marriage would be annulled.

What, then, is the status of these Talmudic presumptions? Are they alterable?

If Rackman believed generally that *hazakot* were historically conditioned observations, rather than "meta-historical" truths, it may be said that he picked a strong example to illustrate his point. For this *hazaka*, which appears in multiple Talmudic contexts and is used as the basis of numerous *halakhot* of marriage and divorce procedure— that is, used as a rationale for making marriage requirements more lax, divorce requirements more strict—is presented by the Talmud itself and understood by later authoritative commentators as being quintessentially of its time and place. The phrase itself has the ring of a folksy rhyming couplet, and Rashi confirms this impression in his gloss, calling it a "popular saying" and emphasizing the physicality of the wording as expressing a strong female point of view: "This is what the women say: 'It is better to dwell with two bodies than as a widow'" (Rashi, BT *Ketubot* 75a, "*tan-du*"). For the women to whom this saying is attributed, simply living alone, whether by divorce or remaining unmarried—one body as opposed to two—was charged with the suffering of widowhood.

In one Talmudic context, this saying is used as a kind of heading for a list of other colorful sayings in a similar vein, reported as being popular among the women of the day:

> A woman is satisfied with any sort [of husband] as Resh Lakish said. For Resh Lakish stated: "It is preferable to live as two than to dwell in widowhood." Abaye said: With a husband [of the stature of an] ant her seat is placed among the great. Rabbi Papa said: Though her husband be a carder, she calls him to the threshold and sits down [at his side]. Rabbi Ashi said: Even if her husband is only a cabbage-head, she requires no lentils for her pot.
>
> (BT KETUBOT 75A)

Taken together, these statements add up to a kind of Talmudic-female gestalt. This impression is fleshed out with increasing vividness in other contexts with considerably heightened stakes. For example, in Talmudic law pertaining to the giving and receiving of binding documents generally, it is permissible for the signatory of a document, in the event that the other party is not physically present, to appoint an emissary to receive it on his or her behalf—so that its effectuation need not be delayed by the receiving party's absence. This halakha, however, carries one key condition: an emissary may only be used to receive a document remotely if the document's outcome is deemed to be beneficial to its recipient. In light of this principle, the Talmud poses the question of whether an emissary may be appointed to receive a *get* on behalf of the woman for whom it is intended. This, of course, merely begs the question: Is divorce considered beneficial to women, in which case it should be permitted to be received remotely and effectuated immediately, even in her absence? Or is it a detriment, in which case it may only take effect when she personally receives it?

The Talmud takes it for granted that, in general, marriage constitutes an advantage to women, if only for socioeconomic reasons. It asks, though, if there may be individual circumstances wherein the quality of a given marriage may be so bad that, all things considered, divorce would still constitute an overall benefit. What about, for example, a woman who is in a marriage that has become quarrelsome—should divorce be considered advantageous to her, such that she be permitted to receive a *get* via emissary? Or should the presumption that she would prefer to be married under any circumstances be applied even then, such that she may only receive her *get* in person—leaving room in the interim, as some commentators suggest, for the likely scenario that when she cools down and her natural preference reemerges, she will change her mind and realize she would rather live in a quarrelsome marriage than live alone? Here again, the Talmud bases its verdict upon the *hazaka*:

> [Is the divorce], since she has a quarrel with her husband, an advantage to her or [is it a disadvantage, since] the gratification of bodily desires is possibly preferred by her? Come and hear what Resh Lakish said: "It is preferable to live as two bodies than to dwell in widowhood."
>
> (BT *Yevamot* 118b)

Palestinian Talmudic sources uphold this principle even in cases of women who find themselves married to degenerate or disease-ridden husbands. Indeed, even in cases in which a woman herself "cries out for a divorce," she is extended no procedural leniency, based on the likelihood that she will come to her senses and change her mind (PT *Gittin* 1:5, 6:1, 5:1; cited in Meiri, *Bet ha-Behira* on BT *Yevamot* 118b, p. 463). Similarly, they made it exceedingly easy for women to marry men suffering from all manner of physical and psychological handicaps that might make it difficult for them to fulfill the obligations detailed in the *ketubah* (marriage contact). The Rabbis simply removed this potential barrier by relieving the male partners of these obligations, announcing, "More than a man wants to marry, a woman wants to be married" (BT *Yevamot* 113a).

For Rackman, these cases all bespeak a kind of social desperation clearly conditioned by historical circumstances. They evoke the world from which they emerged, a world in which for women, simply to be alone invariably constituted a life of suffering and a danger to survival. Why else would a woman be "satisfied with any kind of husband"—even one she has come to despise, whose separation she has come to cry out for? For Rackman, this presumption, while perhaps appropriate for its time—transmitted, after all, in the form of a popular women's jingle—need not necessarily be understood as ever having been intended as a statement of eternal truth. It is perhaps in part the ways in which this *hazaka's* formulation preserves its historical, socioeconomic "personality" that made it a useful test case for the historical and values-based contextualization of inherited *halakha* as a legitimate basis for critique and correction. At the very least, it seemed to him a reasonable candidate for reconsideration.

"Returning the Crown": A Rabbinic Preference for the Past

Rackman, who was known for balancing roles as an establishment figure and gadfly within modern Orthodoxy, would certainly have been aware that he nevertheless faced an uphill battle in his proposal to reevaluate a Talmudic *hazaka*. When he made his proposal at the RCA convention in 1975, he would have been aware of the powerful strains within Rabbinic tradition that privilege the preservation of inherited tradition over potential challenges based on new historical contexts.

We need only recall, for example, the Talmudic passage quoted in chapter 1, in which the Men of the Great Assembly are lauded as "Great" precisely for their ability to "restore the crown of the divine attributes to its ancient completeness" (BT *Yoma* 69b). The prayer that had been spoken by Moses describing a "powerful and awesome" God who triumphs militarily in history no longer resonated for the prophets Jeremiah and Daniel, who lived in times of harsh Jewish defeat and subjugation. Therefore, they omitted these words from their prayers.

> Jeremiah [who prophesied during the destruction of the First Temple] followed and said: Strangers are frolicking in His sanctuary! Where are the displays of His "awesomeness"? Therefore he omitted "awesome" [i.e., he removed it from his prayer]. Daniel [who lived during the Babylonian Captivity that followed the First Temple's destruction] followed and said: Strangers are enslaving His children! Where are the displays of His "power"? And so he did not say "powerful" in his prayer.
>
> (BT YOMA 69B)

While this approach is not rejected by the Talmud, it is considered to be inferior to that invented by the Men of the Great Assembly, who found a way to be truthful while maintaining the words of the more ancient tradition—whose preservation is clearly considered a value unto itself. The Men of the Great Assembly restored the crown of the past by altering the meaning of the language of the past, and herein lies their greatness.

> [The Men of the Great Assembly] followed and said: On the contrary! This is His magnificent strength, for He restrains His will, showing forbearance to the wicked. And these are the displays of His "awesomeness": because, were it not for the awe

[i.e., of the nations] of the Holy One, blessed be He, how could one solitary, singular nation survive among the nations of the world?

(BT YOMA 69B)

The Talmud elsewhere assertively privileges received tradition over reasoned argument. The fate of the convicted "rebellious Elder," who holds on to his own teaching against the ruling of the Sanhedrin, is determined by whether his teaching is based upon tradition—in which case, he lives—or his own logic, in which case he is executed.

In this halakha we find the gravitas of tradition not only foreclosing rational discussion, but in the process literally tipping the balance between life and death. Conversely, a reasoned argument adhered to with conviction literally can get one killed (BT *Sanhedrin* 88a).

A final example will suffice as background to the strong Talmudic tendency to favor the received tradition as a value unto itself, irrespective of what has changed in the conditions of life that made the past legislation necessary or coherent. A paradigmatic instance of this trend can be found in a discussion about the Jewish calendar and the practice, brought about by Rabbinic ordinance, of adding a second, "extra" day of observance to major Jewish festivals celebrated outside of Israel. This practice was initiated in response to a historical circumstance the Talmud sketches in some detail. When the Temple stood, there was no fixed calendar; months would be declared according to when testimony was given by those witnessing the new moon. Months varied in length between twenty-nine and thirty days, depending upon when the testimony was brought and court procedure could allow the moon sighting to be verified. Once the new month was declared by the Sanhedrin, word was sent out to the diaspora by a preordained messaging system that could span great distances quickly. According to the Talmud, that method was eventually sabotaged by heretics, and messengers were sent out instead to deliver the news. It then became impossible to get the word out in time for some of the outlying communities to know when to observe the biblical holidays—hence risking their desecration. In order to remove this doubt, it was instituted for all diaspora communities to observe two days.

I report all of this detail for a reason: to illustrate how contingent upon its historical circumstance was the two-day festival's institution. In the Talmudic period, the doubt that predicated this practice was abolished altogether: the practice of declaring months through testimony ceased, and the calendar was fixed for all time. Logically, this historic shift into certainty should have eradicated the two-day festival observance, which no longer had any practical use. However, the practice was maintained. This struck at least one Talmudic rabbi as strange, and he asked why the extra day had been preserved despite the disappearance of its reason for having been instituted. The question is answered by the anonymous, authoritative voice of the Talmudic editor:

> Because they sent a message from there [i.e., from Israel to Babylonia]: Be cautious in [preserving] the custom of your fathers that is in your hands.
>
> (BT BEITZAH 4B)

Based upon this principle of preciously guarding "the custom of your fathers that is in your hands," two-day observance is maintained even though there is no doubt for anyone, anywhere about when months begin and end. The fact that it was done in the past is enough to justify its preservation, overshadowing in relevance the fact that the ground for the law is no longer applicable. If in the previous source received tradition trumped reasoned argument, here it trumps reality itself. Reality lacks the ability to alter long-standing tradition; the weight of past custom proves far more constitutive of meaning, and thus determinative of ritual practice, than any present reality. We have no doubt, yet live as those who did.

Soloveitchik's "Credo"

Perhaps Rackman, in making his proposal to solve the *aguna* problem by reconsidering a Rabbinic *hazaka*, ultimately hoped he could acknowledge the weight of the past-oriented strain of halakhic tradition while claiming that *hazakot* fall outside the grasp of its preservationist impulse. In any event, it is unlikely that he expected the swiftness or public vehemence with which both he and his proposal were attacked by Soloveitchik shortly after its delivery at the Rabbinical Council of America (RCA) convention in 1975.[7] Soloveitchik was not scheduled to address Rackman's proposal at the convention. Rather, he somewhat dramatically interrupted his own halakhic lecture on another topic to address it, explaining that it saddened him to do so but he felt he had no choice. For Rackman's proposal, as he went on to explain, had violated his very "credo" about the nature of Torah, Torah study, and the God of revelation.

Soloveitchik begins his response to Rackman by emphasizing that Torah study is not an intellectual act alone, but "an ecstatic, metaphysical performance." He provides a stirring experiential account of the role of Torah study and Torah teaching in his own life and its effect upon him: "When I teach, time comes to a stop for me ... teaching has a very strange impact upon me. I simply feel, when I teach Torah, I feel the breath of eternity on my face." For Soloveitchik, Torah study invokes the spiritual presence of God. This experience leads to a cathartic, uplifting effect that provides a sense of comfort from loss and loneliness and wards off depression and dread. But this power of Torah study to overcome death and loss is dependent, according to Soloveitchik, upon our "surrender" of normal or "everyday" human thinking.

> And the study of the Torah is an act of surrender.... What do we surrender to the Almighty? We surrender two things, in my opinion. We surrender up to the Almighty the everyday logic. Or what I call the mercantile logic, or the logic of the businessman. Or the logic of the utilitarian person. And we embrace another logic—*mi'Sinai* ["from Sinai"; revelatory logic]. And secondly, we also surrender the everyday will—which is very utilitarian, very superficial. And we embrace another will. The will *mi'Sinai*.[8]

Within this theology, humans should not expect the logic and will of revelation to mirror their own rational minds and desires. The study of Torah must be approached as a hermetic, self-affirming system, its truths exclusively "obtained from within, in accordance with the methodology given to Moses and passed down from generation to generation." No new approach could possibly add any relevant knowledge to what already has been discovered by the great minds of Rabbinic tradition.

> The truth can be discovered only through joining the ranks of the traditional sages [*hakhmei ha-mesora*]. It's ridiculous to say, "I have discovered something which the Rashbo didn't know, and which the Ketzos didn't know, the Vilna Gaon had no knowledge." [The claim that] "I have discovered an approach to the interpretation of Torah which is completely new!" It's ridiculous. One is to join the ranks of the traditional sages....[9]

The only valid way to learn is to negate the subjective mind in total identification with great scholars of previous generations. This, for Soloveitchik, is the type of Torah study with the potential to lead to the self-contained experience of God's presence he described that introduces the metaphysical possibility of transcending death and loss. To allow what he classifies as a "secular system of values" to guide a halakhic critique spells, for him, an interruption in the self-affirming, revelatory dimension of Torah study, a kind of rude awakening from the dream of divine intimacy—a defeat of revelation's purpose and a slap in the face of God.

> You must not judge laws and ordinances (*hukim u-mishpatim*) in terms of a secular system of values. Such an attempt, be it historicism, be it psychologism, be it utilitarianism, undermines the very foundations of Torah and tradition (*u-mesora*). And leads eventually to the most tragic consequences of assimilationism and nihilism. No matter how good the intentions are of the person who suggests it.[10]

Within this requirement of intellectual surrender, Soloveitchik pointedly requires an acceptance of the infallibility of the Talmudic Rabbis as a halakhically ordained leap of faith. Anyone who might attempt to question or even contextualize either these Rabbis' values ("we must not develop an inferiority complex … one must not try to gear the halakhic norm to the trenchant values of a neurotic society"); their character (we must "revere and love and to admire the words of traditional sages"), or their authority ("They are the final authorities. And irresponsible statements about the sage borders—I don't like to use the word—on the heretical") has already transgressed a theological redline.

This series of premises culminates in a leap that, while far from inevitable, Soloveitchik presents as obvious:

> Not only the *halakhos*, but also the *hazakos* which the traditional sages have introduced, are indestructible. For the *hazakos* which the Rabbis spoke of rest not on trenchant psychological patterns, but upon *permanent ontological principles* rooted in the very depth of the human personality—in the metaphysical human personality—which is as changeless as the heavens above. [emphasis added][11]

Here, Soloveitchik takes a deceptively radical turn, making the acceptance of Talmudic presumptions as "permanent ontological principles" essentially into a criterion of membership in the halakhic community—and labeling anyone who would question them a heretic. He then applies this principle directly to the presumption addressed in Rackman's *aguna* proposal:

> Let's take an example. The *hazaka* for instance—that's what I was told about—the *hazaka* of "better to dwell with two bodies than to dwell as a widow" (*dan le-mesav tan-du mi-lemesav armelu*)—has absolutely nothing to do with the social and political status of the woman in antiquity. The *hazaka* is based not upon sociological factors, but upon a verse in [Genesis]: "I will greatly multiply thy pain … and thy desire

shall be for thy husband, and he shall rule over thee." It is a metaphysical curse, rooted in the feminine personality. She suffers incomparably more than the male while in solitude. Solitude to the male is not as terrible an experience, as horrifying an experience, as solitude to a woman. *And this will never change* ... cause it's not a psychological fact, it's an existential fact. It's not due to the status of the woman, but it's due to the difference, to the basic distinction, between the female personality and the male personality. Loneliness frightens the woman, and an old spinster's life is much more miserable and tragic than the life of an old bachelor. And this was true in antiquity, it is still true, and it will be true 8,000 years from now. So to say that *tam du le-meisav almna* was due, or is due, to the inferior political or social status of the woman, means simply misinterpreting the *hazaka* of *tam du me-lemeisav almna*. And no legislation can alleviate the pain of a single woman. No legislation can change this role. [emphasis added][12]

Based as they are on the ontological status of the woman, not only this Talmudic presumption, but all the halakhic decisions that flow from it, remain permanently and uniformly fixed in place. Neither the passing of time nor the shifting of culture may have any impact upon them whatsoever. Why should they? Historical trends, "trenchant" as they may be, are ultimately capricious, while Talmudic trends reflect unchanging metaphysical truths.

For Soloveitchik, this theology of halakhic permanence lies at the core of his meta-halakhic stance. So central is it to his conception of halakhic integrity, that to question it is literally to court the destruction of the entire system.

And let me ask you a question: God Almighty, if you should start modifying and reassessing the *hazakos* upon which a multitude of *halakhos* rest, you will destroy *yahadus*! So instead of philosophizing, let us rather light a match and set fire to the basis ... there are certain postulates—a certain system of postulates—to which people are committed.... And to speak about changing *hazakos* of *hazal*, of course, is at least as non-sensical as discussing communism at the Republican National Convention. It's discussing methods of self-destruction and suicide....[13]

Soloveitchik makes it incumbent upon all halakhic Jews to view contemporary women in much the same light as the women of the Talmudic era. He insists that the halakhic implications of this identification remain steadfast, claiming that this trans-historical stability is based upon an ontological fact. If the reality you encounter throughout the course of your life seems to fly in the face of this "fact," it is your perception of reality that is to be sacrificed.

In other words, according to Soloveitchik, if you think you are meeting a modern, independent, self-sufficient single woman, dignified about her capacity to cope with reality, you are mistaken: it is an illusion. You are not seeing the real woman, the desperately lonely and abject Talmudic woman that lies at the ontological heart of even the most seemingly capable or contented single modern female. In reality, every powerful, yet-unmarried CEO would prefer a man who has the stature of an ant to the howling pain of singlehood; the professor of history would just as soon live with a cabbage-head or a degenerate. Within this halakhic theology, simply allowing ourselves to acknowledge the reality of what we see is to undermine the foundations of Torah itself. The Torah can only survive if it is based upon what we know not to be true.

The infallibility principle effectively extends divine legitimacy to everything in the Talmud, which becomes no longer the dynamic product of human creativity but a secure, permanent, God-given system that can be relied upon forever. And here we find the deep attraction of the meta-halakhic approach advanced so passionately, and aggressively, by Soloveitchik. Within his paradigm, received halakha constitutes an eternally valid system, offering the security of one who stands outside of history. But it is a security born from blindness, an abnegation of one's subjective experience of reality and a denial of what one sees and knows.

Soloveitchik's Price of Revelation

Rabbi Soloveitchik's public condemnation of Rackman and his proposal achieved its goal—to foreclose consideration of Rackman's *aguna* proposal by mainstream American Orthodoxy and further marginalize Rackman himself. As Soloveitchik's student, pondering this pivotal episode in American Orthodoxy, I must confess both puzzlement and grave disappointment. I live with the fond memory of a teacher unintimidated by any ideas or by any authority—in stark contrast to the other Lithuanian Torah scholars I had studied with.

I will never forget when Rabbi Soloveitchik introduced me to the work of the German Lutheran theologian Rudolph Otto, to help me gain an understanding of prayer. An intellectual giant unafraid to engage with any idea, irrespective of its source, Soloveitchik encouraged his students to explore philosophy or other ideas "alien" to the tradition. He sat in class with total confidence in the ability of Torah to encounter any idea from any culture. I had never heard the head of Lakewood Yeshiva, the great American Orthodox Talmudic academy where I also studied for some time, refer to any thinker outside of the traditional society. To the contrary, at Lakewood I was told to keep my eyes trained at all times on the past.

One incident that encapsulates this ethos is forever etched into my mind. A fellow Lakewood student who had formerly studied in the Kletzk yeshiva, in Belarus, stepped up to lead the rest of us in the afternoon prayer wearing a heavy coat. It was the height of summer in New Jersey, upwards of 100 degrees. I asked him, given the heat, why he had decided to wear a coat. He replied, "In Kletzk, we davened *Mincha* [i.e., prayed the afternoon service] with a coat." I said, "In Kletzk, it was snowing!" But for him, the temperature—the reality of the place in which he stood—was far less relevant than the nostalgia for reality as it once had been.

Soloveitchik, to the contrary, guided me into a future of open-ended intellectual possibility. More than anyone, he is responsible for liberating my mind from the narrow, provincial yeshiva-world mentality and offering me new possibilities for intellectual creativity. As a teacher, he was also intellectually undaunted in the face of authoritative Jewish sources that might disagree with him. I recall one instance during his Talmud class in which a student quoted an authoritative medieval sage in contradiction to the Rav's opinion. Soloveitchik retorted that if that rabbi were sitting in his class now, he would throw him out. It is therefore quite striking for me to hear that same voice claim that anyone who imagines to know something that was unknown to the Rashbo—a sage who lived in medieval Spain—suffers from stupidity. Can we gain a true understanding of the tradition only through the eyes of ancestors who lived in vastly different times than we do? Am I required to learn the same way as the Rashbo; did he and his cohort fix the only legitimate method of Talmudic study?

As it happens, I have developed my own preferred method of halakhic analysis, focusing on the key value distinctions being argued for in legal debates. I do not claim that the medieval commentators have to bow before my autonomous intellect or that I am smarter than they were—just that the problems they faced are not mine. I don't consider myself superior, just different: living in a different culture in which different issues surface and values emerge that were not present in the context of the Rashbo. A historicist orientation to the Talmud was alien to him, whereas I want to use Greek and Roman sources to understand the Talmud's treatment of women. This need not be synonymous with a rejection of traditional forms of learning or the scholars of the past. It certainly seems strange for a man who opened the whole Western tradition to his students to have suggested otherwise.

Whatever its source or motivation, I am in total disagreement with this perception of Torah. The notion of an unchanging presumption of how human beings live their lives might seem dubious under any circumstances. Tying such a presumption to the lives lived and meanings made by women of the Talmudic period, and making that presumption the paradigm for understanding women in the modern condition, stretches credibility to a breaking point—and likely, as Rackman argues, was never intended to be applied in the first place with such "meta-historical" breadth. What is the source, we might ask, of this impulse to stand above history, to feel that halakha must be different in kind from, and thus unaffected by, everything else going on in the world? Why nurture the myth that humans are not the ones who shape, interpret, and have to live by halakha? Is it possible we are expected to ignore humanity in order to live by Torah law, to stand above the vicissitudes and inconsistencies of the temporal world?

In my view, such an approach is devastating to halakhic culture. It yields a Torah not rooted in life, emaciating the lived spirit that is meant to shape the law in its evolving applications. It asks of halakhic Jews commitment to systems of law alien to their own sensibilities. Every halakhic commitment then becomes an *akeida*-like experience of self-sacrifice: I have suspended all of my deeply held ethical values; I live by a law in which I have no presence; I am the ghost of a human being who stands in the image of God. In this theology, denying what we know about ourselves is the true religious moment. This seems to me a recipe for disaster. To the extent that we suppress our own reality, observations, and values, we condemn ourselves to spiritual emptiness from within and without. If the system attempts to make us deny what we know, it risks the encroaching sense that it must hang precariously on an irrational thread.

I have a strong intuition that Soloveitchik felt traditional Orthodoxy was losing ground against secular culture in the marketplace of ideas and could only survive by creating a barrier against having it be subject to comparative cultural studies and historical critique. But what is the price paid for this permanence, and who are the personalities and cultures it produces? I hold rather that the more tradition is steeped in the lived reality of the intellectual culture of our time, the more vibrant it becomes, the more it retains our respect. To build ghetto-like mansions to safeguard the tradition is to admit that Judaism cannot survive in an open society. It means choosing the brittle security of a "permanent" system over a system that absorbs and allows itself to be impacted by contemporary life in all its shifting cultural contingency. It means acknowledging that calling the halakhic system "divine" doesn't strengthen it, any more than calling it "human" detracts.

In my view, taking into account our humanity is precisely what God asks the Jewish people to do in covenantal halakha. This is a key point of divergence from Soloveitchik, for whom surrender and self-sacrifice, not empowerment, is the key feature of halakhic spirituality. I believe that God encourages us to expand our intelligence and build a system that takes into account all the changes that have taken place in the world. A human being affirms his or her lived reality and brings it into the presence of God.

For this reason, I find there to be something deeply inhuman in Soloveitchik's approach to halakhic spirituality. Notwithstanding his profound influence on me and my profound gratitude to him as a student, I must part company with a view of halakha that takes it out of history and out of human experience. Is the price of loyalty to deny what I know to be true? Does it tell me I have to put on different eyes? I do not think that loyalty to and love for this tradition requires exiting history, or exiting life.

Which God Will Guide Halakha—Lover of Permanence, or Hater of False Things?

Rackman and Soloveitchik represent two strongly articulated, strongly opposing approaches to halakha. Soloveitchik's approach has the benefit of supplying a strong answer to the question, how do we deal with a world we have no control over? If history is our enemy, if it always has the potential to turn against us— "A new king arose over Egypt …" (Exod. 1:8)—it makes sense to create a theology that frees us from having to respond to the chaos of lived history. Soloveitchik's halakhic theology lifts its practitioners beyond contingency, to a timeless revelatory dimension in which lived experience is stripped of normative relevance or impact. By adopting a worldview that refuses to validate subjective experience of reality over traditional descriptions of reality, we may transcend the human sense of vulnerability to history, contingency, and chaos.

The Talmudic passage quoted above, in which the Men of the Great Assembly are lauded for restoring the words of the liturgy removed by Jeremiah and Daniel, ends on a powerful note. We will recall that these two prophets omitted the words "powerful" and "awesome" from their prayers, because they did not witness God acting powerfully and awesomely in the course of their lived reality of Jewish degradation and defeat. The Men of the Great Assembly saved these words by reinterpreting them in a way that could accommodate reality as it was.

At the satisfactory conclusion of this short narrative, after the traditional liturgy has been saved, the editorial voice of the Talmud interjects a nagging question: *what possible basis or authority could these prophets have had for making such a radical liturgical shift in the first place?* The answer given is that they did not want to "ascribe false things to God." They did not, in other words, want to lie in God's name. It is interesting that the Talmud considers this logic acceptable at all. How could "powerful" and "awesome"—words to which, having been spoken by Moses in the Torah, the tradition ascribes the highest level of prophecy—possibly be construed as lies? They rest on Moses's authority! Surely Jeremiah and Daniel would not have been lying had they continued to utilize the biblical formula in their prayer.

Yet the Talmud validates their omissions and the logic presented as underlying them. In doing so it gives expression to the sensibility that the authority of the past cannot claim our allegiance when it conflicts with the immediate reality of the present. Our experience must not be denied because of the authority of the past. This is an image of a God that wants us *not* to use the authority of the past to lie to Him. The past has to be validated by your lived experience; if it's not, and you say it is, that is a lie. Your reality has to confirm the validity of the language of the past. The God who loves permanence wants us to deny what we experience, while the God who hates lies wants us to give it credence, to incorporate it into our spiritual and ritual lives. Which God will we allow to guide our halakhic development—the God of Rabbinic infallibility, or the God who demands that I be truthful?

Is the woman we see walking the streets today the woman of the Talmud? No authority in the world can convince me that she is; no past authority can make it into a reality. If that sacrifice is what loyalty to tradition means, there is no person who can trust his or her own eyes. Whom do we see before us? May we see them through our own eyes or only through the lens of Talmudic presumptions?

For Soloveitchik, the woman we see before us is and always will be, in many critical respects, the same woman the Talmudic Rabbis saw. The abject desperation, at least, is the same. It doesn't matter how different she looks, what she says or how she seems, what she accomplishes or how she walks in the world. Rackman's halakha is guided by a different image of God. For him, as for me, reality speaks, and the most important question for the present and future vitality of the halakhic way of life is whether or not we will allow ourselves to listen.

6

THE GOD WHO HATES LIES

Choosing Life in the Midst of Uncertainty

The shifting perceptions of women and non-Jews, discussed in the previous chapters, that have accompanied modern egalitarian, pluralistic thinking are two of the most significant historical developments to challenge traditional halakhic categories and assumptions in the modern period. I would suggest that perhaps an even greater challenge to the inherited halakhic system has been the emergence of a sovereign state in the biblical Jewish homeland. The reality of the State of Israel challenges a halakhic system developed largely in exile to reevaluate some of its most deeply embedded attitudes and categories. How does a people relate to a liturgy based largely around the desperate yearning for a return to Zion in an era that has made it possible, with relatively little risk, to do just that? What does it mean for a legal system developed under diasporic conditions of powerlessness to confront the realities of political autonomy and military force? What is the appropriate halakhic response to the realization of this millennia-old dream?

I recall an encounter with a high-school student that concisely illustrates one dimension of this challenge. The student wanted to discuss a special prayer that is inserted into the afternoon service on the holiday of Tisha B'Av, which commemorates the destruction of the First

159

and Second Temples, the conquests of Jerusalem, and the onerous suffering of exile more generally. The prayer is a lament for the woeful state of the conquered city, razed to rubble and emptied of its Jewish inhabitants. It is also a plaintive plea to God for consolation and the eventual return to a rebuilt Jerusalem.

> Comfort, Lord our God, the mourners of Zion, and the mourners of Jerusalem, and the city that is mournful and ruined, humiliated and desolate: mournful without her children, ruined without her dwellings, humiliated without her dignity, and desolate without a single occupant. She sits with covered head like a barren woman who never gave birth … Blessed are You, God, who consoles Zion and rebuilds Jerusalem.

The student came from a religious family, had been educated in the Israeli Orthodox school system, and was halakhically observant. Nevertheless, it struck him as odd, and a bit nonsensical, to say a mournful prayer over the destruction of and exile of his people from the city they had returned to and rebuilt, the city he lived in and thus knew to be very much alive. The words he was required by halakha to speak, the categories it placed before him to contemplate, the mood it urged him to emulate—all of these contradicted his lived experience. He asked me if I thought he should continue to say the prayer, protesting, "It's not the reality!" It sounded as if he had made up his mind, and yet still he stood there, not liberated but rather seemingly paralyzed by this new awareness, unable to follow through on the consequences of his own logic and intuition. "So what's the problem?" I told him I thought he had made a compelling case. "It's written in the siddur!" he responded.

This student faced a dilemma similar to the one the Talmud attributes to Jeremiah and Daniel (see chapters 1 and 5), albeit with the value poles inverted. Like those prophets, he inherited a liturgical language out of sync with current unavoidable realities. They, having witnessed the destruction of Zion and its aftermath, no longer could bring themselves to describe God as "awesome" or "powerful" in His role as Israel's physical protector. My student, living now in a flourishing Jerusalem, under the protection of an Israeli army, was having a difficult time bringing himself to describe the city as "mournful without her children, ruined without her dwellings, humiliated without her dignity, and desolate without a single occupant." In neither case was the resistance to employing established liturgy motivated by a desire to compromise or diminish the halakhic system. Both, indeed, stemmed from the desire to validate their experience of historical reality and for that experience to be reflected, not contradicted, in the life of prayer. Both, in other words, originated in the halakhic impulse to serve a God who hates lies.

Halakhah and the Reality of the State of Israel

It is not only certain aspects of the liturgy that beg reexamination by the living reality of the Jewish state. Other implications of the Jewish people's decision to organize politically as a sovereign nation should be given normative weight and normative expression by the halakhic system as well. This pressing need for engaged halakhic *response* to an event of sweeping historical impact for the Jewish people extends to basic categories of Jewish identity.

The following story poignantly illustrates the extent to which the current halakhic establishment has failed (or refused) to respond to the reality of Israel. An officer in the Israeli army who had immigrated from Ukraine told me that back home he had been deeply connected to Judaism, "a traditional Jew." Since coming to Israel, he had left religion altogether. This development was not a cause for celebration—his face fell as he described his estrangement from Jewish tradition as "losing it all." What was it, I asked him, that had turned him away?

He proceeded to tell me about a dear friend and comrade, a brave tank-corps officer who had died in battle. When the time came to bury him, the Israeli Rabbinate intervened with a halakhic barrier: in order to be buried in a Jewish cemetery, with full burial rites and rights, they insisted on a rigorous investigation to confirm the Jewish purity of his lineage. Combing through the heroic soldier's family yearbook, they discovered that one of his grandmothers, back in Ukraine, had not been Jewish. For generations the family had lived Jewishly; however, the vicissitudes of their historical situation led to some detours from a direct Jewish bloodline. In the midst of these gaps in "blood Judaism," there was a "living Judaism" that continued uninterrupted.

Sadly, if unsurprisingly, the Rabbinate gave no weight to these considerations of historical context when determining the level of respect with which this fallen soldier would be honored, in death, by the country and the people for whom he gave his life. Nor did they give any normative status to the striking fact itself that this young man, self-identified as a Jew, had died a death defined *quintessentially* by loyalty to his country and his people. To the Rabbinate, populated mostly by ultra-Orthodox non-Zionists who openly reject any attempt to acknowledge (much less respond to) the reality of the State of Israel within halakha, the blemish in his pedigree was sufficient to disqualify him from a full Jewish burial. He was banished to a corner of the cemetery reserved for non-Jews—a public denial of the identity he had claimed for himself while alive, and a forced estrangement from the very people whose destiny he had joined and whose survival he had fought and died to continue.

As the officer who had known him related this story to me, he became enraged.

"How could Israel ask me to die for it as a Jew," he demanded to know, "*then not bury me as a Jew?*" I looked at him and saw his pain, which was a pain for the loss and terrible posthumous humiliation of his friend, and which also, I sensed, contained an element of deep personal suffering for the small-minded ways in which Jewishness is being defined in his country. For it was not the horror of his friend's death that caused him to reject Jewish tradition, but the horrifying insensitivity with which he was treated by the Rabbinate after he was gone. Concluding his story, the officer asked me, how *could* he be loyal to the tradition when it was capable of such a callous betrayal?

I could not really argue with him. This did indeed seem to be an instance in which the halakhic system had failed to formulate a constructive response to the complex, emerging social realities of Jewish life in Israel—with devastating consequences.

We have noted a powerful trend within modern halakhic theology to hold the halakhic system aloof in principle from any influence based on shifts in historical reality. Dominant currents within Orthodoxy hold fast to Talmudic perceptions of women and non-Jews despite a surplus of visible evidence to the contrary. Yet the remarkable fact remains: the Jewish people have decided to become, once again, a political force in history. What is the appropriate halakhic response to this radical shift in historical reality? Can halakhic formalism and idealism fence off the emergence of an entire nation?

Who Is the Authentic Israel?

Sadly, as I have seen demonstrated again and again throughout my decades of living in Israel, the answer to this last question is yes. The Israeli *haredi* (ultra-Orthodox) community has staked its very self-definition on the rejection of historical reality as a legitimate factor in halakhic development. The notion that the establishment of a modern Jewish political state in Israel could have any religious significance—much less that it might impinge in any way on established halakha—is decried as heresy. In my view, this proud estrangement from the collective will and spirit of the Jewish people, the contemptuous detachment from its historical drama, deeply weakens this community's claim as an authentic mediator of halakhic tradition.

I will never forget a call I received from my daughter on Yom Hazikaron, Israel's Memorial Day. The holiday is commemorated by a two-minute-long air-raid siren at eleven in the morning, during which it is customary for everyone in the country to stop what they are doing—even drivers pull their cars over to the side of the road—and stand in silence. My daughter sounded disoriented and upset on the phone, explaining that she had been in a *haredi* neighborhood when the siren went off. She was shocked to witness the people around her exhibiting no reaction or response to the siren, carrying on about their daily business as if nothing were happening at all. Intellectually, of course, she knew that *haredi* policy was not to acknowledge the siren—their official explanation being that it constitutes a "gentile" form of commemoration, and thus a violation of the halakhic prescription not to "emulate the customs of the [gentile] nations" (Lev. 18:3). Nevertheless, the total indifference to a nation giving expression to two minutes of mourning was dumbfounding and deeply disturbing to her; she simply could not imagine that she was in Israel.

I tried to calm her by explaining that her intuition was correct: in an important sense, she was *not* in Israel. According to Maimonides, there is a category of person who may be fully observant in the sense of not transgressing, but nevertheless "separates himself from the community of Israel, and does not do mitzvot in their midst, and does not enter with them into their suffering, and does not fast on their fast days, but rather walks about his way like one of any other nation, and acts as if he is not *of* them." This person, Maimonides informs us, however externally religious he may seem, is classified as a *poresh mi-darkei tzibur*—literally, "one who separates oneself from the ways of the community"—and stripped of his portion in the World to Come.

In my opinion, those who use halakha as a shield against history to justify their refusal to acknowledge the State of Israel, much less allow its religious significance to inform halakhic development—these people have severed themselves from the historical drama of the Jewish people. Those who use halakha to justify their refusal to participate in the army or accept their share of the economic burdens of the society—these are the true secular Jews of this country. No matter how many mitzvot they perform, no matter how many transgressions they avoid, they operate in conscious isolation from the broader community of Israel. They "do not enter with them into their suffering … but rather [walk] about [their] way like one of any other nation, and [act] as if [they are] not of them." These are the true *porshim* (pl.) *mi-darkei tzibur*. Their fate, according to Maimonides, is not to be admired.

I once shared this opinion with a *haredi* yeshiva boy—that by not caring about the security and economic welfare of the State of Israel, his community had isolated itself from the community of Israel and earned the classification of *porshim*. He became upset and shot back that it is precisely the greater secular society, who do not observe Torah and mitzvot, who are the *porshim*. The *haredi* community, he said, were the true *shomrei gahelet*: the dedicated and dutiful keepers of the smoldering ember of Jewish tradition. Without *us*, he said, Judaism would cease to exist in this country, and the fire of the Torah would be lost, and with it, the Jewish people's entire reason for being.

It was then I realized that the complicated secular-religious debate in Israel revolves ultimately around one central question: who is to be considered "the *tzibur*/community"? Who represent legitimate expressions of Jewish collective life such as to be considered authentic bearers of the Jewish story? Is it the army officers who expose their lives to danger? The kibbutzniks, immersed in safeguarding the society's agricultural well-being? The politicians and professors? Or is it those who reject the possibility of religiously significant events occurring in history—who view all of the above as, in essence, Jewish only by chance, performing actions of no relevance to received tradition and thus no consequence to the true Jewish story?

The oft-asked question "Who is a Jew?" has been given more prominence than it deserves; in many ways it is beside the point, a red herring of communal discourse. Its real value is that it points to a much larger and more serious question: who are the Jewish people today? What community is considered as having the authority to interpret, apply, and reshape tradition as it passes through our lifetimes—to make, as in the "Who is a Jew?" example, core decisions about the parameters of Jewish identity? Who is the *tzibur*? Israel, and the Jewish people as a whole, are divided on this fundamental fault line. A small, active, vocal segment of the population consider themselves to be the exclusive authentic Israel. I consider those who are prepared to die for the continuity of the Jewish story, while creating a society with conditions of health and economic well-being, to have a much stronger claim as the true carriers of Jewish history.

I once spoke to a *haredi* friend who was about to board an El Al flight to Israel. "On your way back to *Medinat Yisrael* [the State of Israel]"? I asked him. "No," he replied—he was going to *Eretz Yisrael* (the Land of Israel). With this pointed distinction, common among non- and anti-Zionist *haredim*, he was asserting that the fact that Jews have gathered to create a new state for themselves in their ancestral homeland has no meaning for him—no more meaning than a group of incidental Jews gathering as a community in Florida, or Wisconsin, or Kathmandu. For him, the building of one *kollel*—where married men engage in full-time Talmud study, supported financially by donors and, in Israel, by the state—carries far more significance than the building of a "secular" state. I tried to call his bluff, asking him if he would still be willing to live in Israel if every adult man studied in *kollel*, leaving no one to build the economy, serve in the military, or run the state. But he called my bluff instead, answering, "Absolutely! Because then I *know* we'd be secure." It was hard to imagine a more vivid illustration of the disconnection of the religious life from even the most seemingly basic conception of reality.

Similarly, I sometimes informally poll *haredi* yeshiva boys as to whether they celebrate Yom Ha'atzmaut (Israeli Independence Day) with prayers of *hallel* (praise) and *hoda'ah* (thanksgiving). The answer is always no; in other words, they are saying, we give no religious weight to this reality. They are willing to take advantage of the health and security conditions that the Jews who are invested in it provide, but unwilling to assign these "services" any intrinsic moral or religious value. The true normative Israel for them was, is, and always will be those who carry the banner of a super-historical Torah.

But of course, this assertion itself only begs the question: What is the Torah today? Can we really stomach the claim that halakha today is exactly the same as it was two thousand years ago or two hundred years ago? Previous generations of sages and communities rose to meet the challenges posed by radical shifts in historical circumstance with theological creativity and halakhic innovation, honoring both the vital inheritance of tradition and the demands and opportunities of the living society. The denial of the impact of historical reality on religious consciousness—and the rejection of change it feeds and reinforces—is not the only option the tradition makes available to us, despite heated claims to the contrary espoused by various streams of Orthodox theology. There is nothing to prohibit us from soberly asking ourselves: Has a new value emerged in history, the value of a living Jewish people who want to build a total collective society? Is Israel an authentic community for mediating the Jewish story? We need no permission, in other words, to see what is in front of our eyes. And so, if we insist that our living halakha resist "ascribing false things to God"—if we allow it to be mediated by the God who hates lies—the Torah that has sustained the Jewish people in its meandering path through history will continue its evolution in response to the normative needs of this sovereign Jewish collective.

For if the reality of Israel demands a sweeping halakhic response, the meaning we ascribe to that reality will guide the direction of the response. I propose that a core meaning of the State of Israel is precisely the will of the Jewish people to remain in history, despite overwhelming evidence of the risks involved. In the face of a punishing experience of exile culminating in the Holocaust, the decision not to run away, but to place oneself on the front lines, literally and figuratively, of history's vicissitudes and vulnerabilities—war, violence, poverty, oppression—embodies a religious statement of defiant optimism so powerful that it cries out for a normative response. The life-affirming decision to reconstitute ourselves as a nation in response to the Shoah demands an affirming response from the tradition in return. For non-Jews to join the Jewish people in a post-Shoah world, in which our safety cannot be taken for granted and our communities are embattled both from within and without, reverberates with religious meaning. To join this people at this moment in history is an act infused with covenantal value. This decision should merit recognition in some form of halakhic membership status.

It is for this reason that when the secular Israeli soldiers who study at my institute ask me how I see their Jewishness—they are used to Orthodox rabbis telling them they are not Jewish or, at least, not Jewish enough—I tell them that their lives are an embodiment of the will to keep Jewish history alive. I do not patronize them by claiming that this is their conscious intention or goal. I do not claim that the State itself has any intrinsic holiness—but that the impulse to maintain and defend and nurture it does, and thus the role that they play as guarantors of Jewish history speaks for itself. This alone, in my opinion, gives them enormous religious status, and this status should be recognized both theologically and halakhically.

And it is for this reason that I find the image of a *haredi* Rabbinate delegitimizing the Jewishness of a soldier killed while protecting the citizens of the Jewish state from harm—those very religio-crats among them—mind-boggling and utterly repellant. Inherited halakha may define the fallen soldier discussed above as a nonmember, and contemporary rabbis indifferent to the reality of Israel may promptly bury their heads in the sand, insisting that halakha provides no mechanism by which to mitigate his outsider status. For them, traditional mitzvot are the only category that mediate brotherhood—and they are the only community permitted to mediate the meaning and practice of mitzvot. They are the *tzibur*, the authentic bearers of the tradition, and their version of mitzvah-brotherhood constitutes its sole legitimate expression.

I strongly believe that we live in an era in which self-identification, combined with an embodied commitment to the continuity of Jewish history, constitutes a critical mediating category of Jewish identity and that this recognition should be incorporated into the halakhic system in some form of membership status. I assign serious religious weight to the willingness to stay in history, to build and cultivate and defend and die in order to sustain a nation's vitality and survival. This lived commitment itself carries major religious significance from a covenantal perspective. It is, in itself, one of the most significant religious acts a person can perform in the modern world, and it is an act that should provoke a commensurate response from the halakhic system. The question of how to express its religious gravitas normatively, in the laws of conversion, reflects the type of halakhic thinking we should allow this new reality to inspire.

For example, in my opinion, the brave young Israeli soldier killed in battle should have been granted full status as a Jew and been buried in a Jewish cemetery with not only full military honors, but all the rights and privileges extended by halakha to the Jewish dead. I do not understand this as an antinomian impulse—that inherited halakha should simply be factored out. To the contrary, the halakhic response in this case must be guided by the moral considerations implicit in the question of which image of God we intend to serve through our halakhic practice. A response mediated by the God who hates lies might draw upon the paradigm of circumcision, the drawing of blood that constitutes entrance into the covenant, a marker of membership for Jewish males and a condition of (male) conversion. This cut, the *dam brit* (blood of the covenant) affirms a willingness both to live and, if necessary, to sacrifice oneself for the sake of Jewish continuity—always to conceive of oneself, in part, as a link in the chain advancing the covenantal community toward its ultimate destiny. What ritual status might be extended to Israeli soldiers fighting on the front lines to protect the covenantal communities of Ashkelon and Ashdod, putting their very bodies on the line as living exemplars of the *dam-brit* ethos?

A halakha that is alive to the historical moment might draw upon the archetypal example of Ruth, whose defiant proclamation of solidarity with Jewish peoplehood made her a cornerstone of Rabbinic thinking about conversion. Her courageous act of identification ("Your people shall be my people" [Ruth 1:16]) resonates with special poignancy in Israel and in the post-Holocaust world more broadly (I will elaborate upon this latter dimension more fully below). Maimonides, in a passage describing conversion procedure, gives a ruling that seems guided by this spirit:

> How are religious converts received? When a person comes to convert, and is investigated and no ulterior motives are found, say to him or her: "Why do you want to convert? Don't you know that the Jewish people, in these times, are distressed and persecuted and oppressed and harried and afflicted?" If the person says, "I know, and I am not worthy"—*receive him or her immediately.* [emphasis added][1]

Jewish tradition possesses no shortage of resources with which to formulate a creative response to issues of Jewish identity status. What is lacking is a *tzibur* that sees itself as both empowered and willing to use them.

Conversion: A Process of Experiential Education

It is not only in death that the collective will to remain in history manifested by Israel should impact halakha's formulation of Jewish identity status. The new ways in which the living reality of a total Jewish society mediates the lived experience of being Jewish—most intensively for Israelis, but also for Jews worldwide—should find expression in the ways Jewish identity is formulated in both the public discourse and the practical halakha of conversion.

For example, the dominance of "authority" in the public discourse about conversion grates painfully against the very meaning and spirit of the new reality of Israel. Embracing history, with all its vagaries and contingencies, in the fullest sense of collective responsibility and individual dignity—this powerful stance calls for a powerful response. This should include shifting our halakhic focus, when it comes to defining membership, from questions of purity and authority to the health and benefit of the living community.

As noted above, Maimonides viewed the conscious, willing identification with the Jewish people as the primary criterion for conversion—a potential resource in a reexamination and reformulation of a conversion law unafraid to respond to the emergent reality of Israel. One might object that halakha also makes conversion contingent upon the acceptance of mitzvot, participation in the spiritual life of the community as mediated by its symbols and rituals. Communal discourse around the meaning of this requirement, in particular, has been dominated by bitter internecine battles over authority—precisely the question of who most authentically claims the mantle of *tzibur* and who may thus define the meaning of mitzvot acceptance. Orthodox factions, particularly *haredi* non- and anti-Zionists, have defined the commitment to "receiving the mitzvot" in increasingly narrow ways, making standards for conversion prohibitively strict and arcane as a way of aggrandizing authority to themselves as the sole true arbiters of authentic Jewishness. The notion of binding the convert to the Jewish nation broadly speaking is irrelevant. For them, the only acceptable conversion is one that affirms absolute loyalty to their niche communities, which for them constitute the only *tzibur* relevant for consideration of any kind.

One perverse outgrowth of this authority fetish has been the trend of retroactive negation of conversions. Let's say a Jew converted within an Orthodox framework is spotted in a non-kosher bakery. It doesn't matter how much time has passed, be it months or decades. If the information is brought to a rabbinic authority who takes an interest in it (in the last decade, an increasingly likely response), that authority may retroactively invalidate the conversion. If the convert is a woman, and she has in the meantime built a Jewish family, any of her children are immediately stripped of their Jewish status. No matter if they have lived their entire lives as Jews; no matter to what extent they have demonstrated a commitment to Jewish identity and peoplehood. This is obviously an ugly and unacceptable circumstance. Moreover, it is possible for all of the conversions of a given rabbi to be annulled retroactively if that *rabbi's* status is somehow compromised. This has happened, families left reeling with a sweeping wave of the halakhic establishment's callous hand. Again, considerations of lived practice simply do not register on the scale of religious value. It is a terrible and destructive irony that the majority of those legislating Jewish status in Israel, for the rest of the Jewish world, attribute no religious significance to the willingness to live and die for the continuity of Jewish history.

It is not only the extreme consequences of the halakhic infatuation with authority, such as retroactive conversion, that prove destabilizing and demoralizing to contemporary Jewish life. Denominationalism generally is a cancer eating away at the authenticity of Judaism both in Israel and the diaspora. Framing halakha as a rigid zero-sum game effectively disqualifies it as a "live option" for the vast majority of living Jews. My son recently related to me two disconcerting stories that speak directly to this theme of assigning undue value to considerations of authority versus lived experience.

Both members of a couple had converted to Judaism. Since their conversion they had had children and raised an active Jewish family, as committed members of the synagogue who sent their children to Jewish day schools. It came about that the religious educator at the day school their son was attending discovered that one of the rabbis who had presided over their conversion had been Conservative. The educator, who was Orthodox, promptly decreed that the boy was not Jewish—that he was suddenly, in every relevant way, to be perceived by everyone else at the school as gentile. The educator reinforced this message by henceforth excluding the boy from being counted in the minyan of his peers; pointing out that the ritual objects he was making in arts and crafts were *treyf*, having been fashioned by the hands of a gentile; and when his class returned from a field trip just before the arrival of Shabbat, being asked to turn the lights on and off, making him into a resident *Shabbes goy*, contemptuously ignoring his life's record as an active, committed Jew.

These incidents occur often, and they are a blot on the integrity of the Jewish people.

Despite how he and his family lived, despite their integrity and sincerity in identifying with the covenant of Moses, this boy was publicly humiliated and ostracized because the conversion was not performed by three Orthodox rabbis. It is almost too painful to imagine the undeserved suffering of this boy who had acted and seen himself as a good Jew his entire life and whose family's profound commitment to Jewish tradition had been twisted into the cruelest kind of joke. How can a people equated with light bring such darkness even to their own?

The source of this particular darkness is, to me at least, fairly clear. It is the myopic and misguided focus on *who does* the conversion, rather than *what type of person* is standing before you—much less anything about how they actually happen to live. It is insisting that issues of authority and legitimacy eclipse the living spirit of Judaism that this family, for example, had practiced for over twenty years. It is the refusal to give credence to history and lived reality out of a desire to maintain exclusive authority as the system's legitimate mediator, combined with the false idea that having standards of authority will guarantee that the conversion has authenticity, rather than the quality of a person living and learning within the Jewish people. The anxious, hostile jockeying over denominational labels per se; the monopolistic, self-satisfied, self-aggrandized power that the Orthodox Rabbinate has assumed for itself—none of this has anything to do with the lived reality of the Jewish people. And whether the presiding rabbi is Conservative or Reform says nothing about the sincerity of the convert in his or her desire to join that people and become a part of that reality.

The Jewish-communal affirmation of life in response to the Shoah has found two powerful primary expressions: the establishment of Israel, and the re-creation of American Jewry in the post-Holocaust era as a proud collective in the public space. The emergence of a self-confident American Jewry after the Shoah is itself a religious act; to identify with the Jewish people is not just a national, but a *covenantal* statement.

To miss the most spiritually potent expressions of living Judaism in millennia seems clearly an affront to this people, and perhaps something closer to a sin. Thus, those who take a rejectionist approach toward converts sin twice over, violating the deep biblical-ethical prohibition against shaming the converts; and emptying of its spiritual value one of the most profound covenantal achievements in Jewish history.

My son also described a discussion he had had with an Israeli soldier. The soldier was not particularly observant, but he was open to experimenting with aspects of Jewish tradition. A few years ago, he had adopted a non-Jewish child with the intention of raising the child as a Jew. When he approached the Israeli Rabbinate about converting the child, they required him to promise that he would raise the child in full accordance with strict halakhic Orthodoxy—send him to yeshiva, strictly observe the laws of Shabbat and kashrut. He said yes, fully aware that he was lying.

Now, he wanted to adopt another child under similar circumstances—with, he told my son, one key difference. He had found the experience of lying before the rabbinic court to be depressing and demoralizing. He desperately wanted and needed the conversion to be validated by the Rabbinate; at the same time, he did not feel he would be able to lie. The soldier was perceptive enough to realize the absurdity of the position he was being put in. *Can I enter the Jewish people with the willingness to learn and experiment and understand?* he had eloquently and indignantly demanded to know. *Can I try on different observances as I come to know this people more and more, by experiencing the way it lives and breathes together? Can Judaism be an educational process for me?*

Finally, this vexed soldier and father was seeking practical advice. "Must I lie in order to adopt a child I intend to raise as a Jew?" My son told him, sadly, that in the current communal climate, unless he wanted to risk the conversion being blocked, the safest path was to misrepresent his religious lifestyle. This dose of the divisive reality of contemporary halakhic politics brought his prospective experiment with Jewish tradition to a close.

Why demand such false totalities? Only a Rabbinate insensitive to the normative implications of Israel could refuse to admit halakha as an ongoing educational process, where connection and commitment can develop in stages, guided by the subjective experience of the seeker. Rather than being constructed as a gatekeeper requiring full loyalty and guaranteeing full certainty, can conversion give expression to a leap into the possible? Can we affirm its value as a move toward an authentic, truthful possibility, what William James would have called a "live option"? Talmudic statements like "One who rejects idolatry fulfills the entire Torah" seem to voice such a welcoming spirit—one that does not set the bar for membership status at immediate fulfillment of the entire Torah, but rather allows for a process to take place.

In my view, Israel allows for a formulation that understands the "receiving of mitzvot" not as a total commitment to the tradition in its entirety as mediated by its strictest, most authoritarian interpreters— but rather, as a process of experiential education (see chapter 2). This interpretation is hinted at in the Talmud, which relates a vignette about a non-Jew who approached Hillel the Elder with a proposition (BT *Shabbat* 31a). He wanted to convert to Judaism on the condition that he would be taught only the Written (i.e., scriptural), but not the Oral (i.e., rabbinically interpreted) Torah. For the Talmud, Rabbinic tradition's canon, the rejection of that tradition—or indeed, any one of its constituent halakhot—constituted heresy and a sound reason for rejecting conversion. This view is reflected in the preceding story, in which the same prospective convert approaches Shammai the Elder with the same condition and is promptly and angrily shooed off.

But Hillel takes a different tack, converting the man on the spot. The medieval commentator Rashi explains Hillel's reason for doing so:

that, in the educational process through which Hillel would guide him, he would become "progressively more accustomed." Hillel, according to Rashi, relied upon this educational process as the means through which the place of authority within the tradition would be better understood and ultimately accepted. What is critical to note here is that he does not make total acceptance of traditional authority a *prerequisite* for conversion. An echo of Hillel's process-oriented approach to conversion can perhaps be found in another Rabbinic source, which reports him as asserting that "one mitzvah leads to another" (*Pirkei Avot* 4:2).

This educational ethos becomes especially relevant in the context of a living Jewish society. The collective environment becomes an educational experience unto itself. Judaism is alive in the streets, with the pulse and the rhythms of a people. In Israel, one need not attend synagogue on Yom Kippur night to know the solemn day has arrived. One smells it in the streets, hears it in the silence, sees it in the sun setting over the walls. This lived reality liberates us to focus our religious attention not on the blunt mechanisms through which authority is consolidated and enforced, but rather on what processes have been set in motion, what sensitivities and sensibilities are being developed—how the melodies of Jewish life resonate within a person's soul.

In short, the spirit of the State of Israel is Jewish peoplehood broadly defined—to welcome without undue concern over the credentials of the legitimating authority. This is the spirit that should inform conversion in Israel and should mediate the discussion and policy of conversion worldwide. It is the spirit in which the Law of Return was initially adopted, though the *haredi* Rabbinate has been working tirelessly to ensure that the letter of the law prevents it from fulfilling its spirit. In my view, the Law of Return is vividly emblematic of the true inclusive spirit that is the meaning of Israel: any Jew who wishes to identify completely with the historical solidarity and continuity of the Jewish people has a home.

The fact that the Law of Return, with its majestically inclusive premise, has become a mechanism of the Orthodox Rabbinate's attempt to delegitimize three-fourths of diaspora Jewry is simply perverse. Their campaign to monopolize authority over all matters of Jewish identity status is antithetical to the covenantal historical destiny of the Jewish people. The focus on exclusive control opposes this people's deepest understanding of its own existence at this moment in history; the desperate and cynical maneuvering to reshape halakha into a private club for fundamentalists reflects a deep failure to identify with this people in this moment. A nation has mustered the courage to affirm their story publicly, to reclaim their covenantal-historical destiny and resist the forces threatening to wipe their story out of history for good.

A Theology of Response

It is important to take a moment to clarify the aspect of my theology that animates this dynamic relationship between halakha and history, or what I might term a theology of response. What is the conceptual basis for investing history with religious significance such that it merits halakhic response? Moreover, readers and critics have often pointed out that imbuing history with religious significance seems at odds with my theological insistence that we can have no access to God's will or plan for history. How can I religiously celebrate the establishment of the State of Israel, for example, when I lack a coherent way of understanding the Holocaust? How can I sing prayers of praise and thanksgiving for the rebirth of sovereign Jewish peoplehood on Yom Ha'atzmaut, yet become silent and dumbfounded the moment I begin to contemplate that people's near annihilation?

This seeming discrepancy is resolved by means of a critical distinction, hinted at in Soloveitchik's *Kol Dodi Dofek*, between the metaphysics or logic of description and the metaphysics or logic of response. I have no way to make sense logically or rationally of a God who remains indifferent to evil perpetrated on such an overwhelming scale. It destroys all rational coherence when one attempts to imagine a God passively supervising the events of the Holocaust. There is no metaphysics that can grasp this howling absence. The logic of description withers and breaks down.

Therefore I must be perfectly clear that halakhic response does not derive from, and should not be equated with, an attempt to give a descriptive account of God's actions in history. When it comes to Israel, I do not base the imperative of halakhic response upon intimations or predictions about which stage of spiritual history Israeli state-building occupies on the path to messianic redemption. There is no predetermined master-narrative of Jewish historical destiny into which I can neatly slot our current era, using this descriptive claim as a justification for halakhic change. To the contrary, I have absolutely no access to the divine plan in history, no way to explain any of God's actions, and no reassuring sense of an inevitable redemption. Even the physical survival of the Jewish people, much less their eventual triumph, is far from guaranteed.

Nevertheless, I am alive in this particular historical moment, endowed with human consciousness, a spiritual community, and a desire for a relationship with God. And so the question persists: how do I respond to the events I witness and participate in during my lifetime? I have argued, in chapter 1, that halakha was framed by Rabbinic tradition as a substitute for the absent God of history, structuring a total reality that provides opportunities to sense the divine presence in every aspect of human experience. I do not claim that halakha acts to instantiate God's presence in a descriptive, metaphysical sense, that it offers or reflects any special understanding of God's actions in history. Rather, it presents the soul who seeks intimacy with his or her God a wide range of opportunities to set that God before one constantly.

Historical developments, while not descriptive of a divine plan, should also not be considered immune to this type of spiritual opportunity. An event took place that marked an amazing change in the Jewish condition of history. The religious significance of this event is rooted not in a metaphysical truth-claim about its place in God's unfolding historical scheme, but in an existential mood: how do I, along with my community, express our joy and gratitude for this remarkable change in our fortunes? When I sing grateful prayers it is not with the intention of thanking God for intervening in history to bring about the Jewish state, but because this momentous event awakens in me an existential response, and the tradition provides me with a spiritual language in which to express it. This is my frame of mind as I recite these prayers.

Living as a Total Communal Entity in History

Thus, while affirming my skepticism at the possibility of understanding or describing divine actions in history, I must also recognize that in the establishment of the State of Israel I have witnessed one of the most radical transformations ever faced by the Jewish people. It is an event pregnant with significance, and this significance calls out to be articulated within the structure of our individual and collective lives. I claimed above that one of the core religious meanings of the State of Israel is the will of the Jewish people to remain alive and present in history. Against the Holocaust's black backdrop, the rebirth of Israel is a profound communal statement: we refuse, the Jewish people announced, to abandon the project of living as a total communal entity in history.

To clarify, I do not mean to suggest that the Jews have been previously absent from history, only entering it now with the emergence of statehood. There are Zionist thinkers who make that claim, but I am not among those who subscribe to it. We have always been in history. New is the degree to which we are responsible and capable of shaping the direction of our collective life: to stand upon the world stage not merely in reaction to events occurring outside of our control, but with a sense of responsibility for the total framework of Jewish experience; to embrace the possibility of autonomously envisioning an open future, with the mechanisms of authority and bureaucracy at hand for implementing it.

We have been in history, but we have also, by necessity, constructed corners of communal life that made it possible to hide. Synagogues, community centers, Federation buildings—these diaspora institutions allow Jews to gather in community in a way that is set apart from the flow of life in the society at large. The natural response of a people having undergone the evil and devastation of the Holocaust would have been to reinforce this tendency, to retreat further into hiding. History has proved itself time and again to be a dangerous place for the Jews; why not find a corner, a niche, to hide out in until the dust clears? We should have gone down to the coffeehouses of history, hiding and assimilating and fading away.

Indeed, my wife and I, as a young couple, went through agonizing discussions about whether or not we had the right to bring a child into the world as a Jew, exposing him or her to such great and proven risk. But no, we decided: the instinct of our people was to go public, to be visible in history, come what may. The Jew no longer runs and hides; we are a people who do not look for an exit whenever we enter a theater. We seek not a portable lifestyle with a flexible escape plan, but a way to anchor ourselves in the world. The will to sustain our lives is a powerful will that animates nearly every aspect of Israeli society. In Jerusalem, *lechayim* (to life) is an everyday greeting.

I once asked the Israeli philosopher and gadfly Yeshayahu Leibowitz *zz"l* what he thought to be the core religious meaning of Israel's establishment. He responded concisely: "Not to be ruled by the goyim." Collective sovereignty further actualizes the human desire for self-rule, which is in turn a desire for dignity, a central value of the Jewish covenant. The opportunity to take responsibility for the health care, security, and economic well-being of a total Jewish society, for its cultural and literary achievements: for this opportunity, and in response to it, Leibowitz—who was not only strictly Orthodox but had no trouble accusing more liberal Jewish movements of, at best, religious narcissism—was himself prepared to demand sweeping changes throughout the halakhic system.

I share Leibowitz's intuition about the religious significance of Israel's experiment in building a total Jewish society. It is why I moved here with my family, why I have stayed, and why I continue, often despite my better judgment, to insert my voice into the chorus of voices battling for a role in envisioning its future. The existential experience I have when I get off an El Al airplane is one of familiarity and intimacy, of deep memories being awakened. I walk the streets of Jerusalem named for my heroes of Jewish history: Isaiah, Maimonides, Hillel. Before each holiday, the supermarkets overflow with the symbolic delicacies and accoutrements of the season.

This all-encompassing environment stands in stark contrast to the experience of collective life outside of Israel. Once, as the holiday of Sukkot approached, I found myself in a supermarket in Berkeley,

California. I asked the owner where I might find kosher food for the holiday meal, and he pointed to a small, remote corner of the store. When my young son walked into an Israeli supermarket for the first time after we had moved here, he expressed an excitement I was also feeling but too "grown-up" to express out loud: "*Abba!* Everything's kosher!"

Similarly, when I walk down the commercial boulevard near my home before and during Sukkot, almost every restaurant features a temporary ritual hut extending out onto the sidewalk—offering the general public way to give expression to the holiday in the course of one's natural daily rhythm. This tremendous opportunity to feel at home—not relegated to a depressing corner of the supermarket—is a marvelous, joyful experience. It does not need to be legitimated with reference to some eternal value, some grand metaphysical truth. Its religious significance is rooted in its impact on my experience. I have come home; I am not a stranger. I must allow my religious life to be mediated by this experience; I must find ways to give it expression within the halakhic framework that in turn mediates my sense of God's presence.

While criticizing certain aspects of Israeli society I find it important to invoke this backdrop of daily joy and celebration. For it is the lived experience that motivates my halakhic vision; it is the experience that creates the opportunity, and the necessity, for halakhic response. I often remind others and myself that when criticizing Israel, one must be critical as a parent: feeling the pain, not rejoicing in it. This society has achieved an enormous breakthrough, creating a home that can be experienced within a total context of Jewish memory and intimacy.

A Light Unto Nations: The Public Face of the Jewish People

It is precisely this achievement that carries with it such inspiring potential and consequently such a rigorous set of demands. While not necessarily sharing their political or religious orientation, I nevertheless strongly identify with those who saw in Israel the potential for a new socialist utopia, manifested in the kibbutzim. I affirm Martin Buber's deep assessment that the kibbutz was an experiment that did not fail. The aspiration to build an egalitarian society with an emphasis on social justice, with a health system in which no human being would be deprived of decent care, with schooling, through the university level, that is affordable for the majority, in contrast to the astronomical cost of an equivalent combined Jewish and general education in the diaspora—these achievements are inspiring to many Jews who relate to its mission as being "a light of nations" (Isaiah 42:6). In a very deep and significant way, Israel is the public face of the Jewish people. If the world seeks to understand who the Jews are, they point to the Jewish state as in some way mediating for them a profounder understanding of the Jewish soul.

By the same token, a society in which Jews are responsible for the totality of life cannot accept a family structure in which men are systemically empowered to dominate women's lives. Such a society cannot tolerate the existence of one *aguna*. A society that seeks justice and dignity for its members cannot, when implementing the Law of Return, make hierarchical distinctions between Orthodox, Conservative, and Reform rabbis. In all matters relating to Jewish identity status, it should give greater credence to the quality of a person's religious life than to the vagaries of ethnic background. Israel should welcome, and the halakhic system should accommodate, all those who feel that building a Jewish home after the Holocaust is today the great mitzvah, and the great challenge, of Jewish life. It should allow membership standards that give normative weight to the willingness to self-identify—to live and potentially to sacrifice—as Jews, and for a conception of halakha as an educational process: an opportunity for those seeking to deepen their connection with God and Jewish peoplehood to do so experientially and experimentally, according to their subjective intuitions and needs.

Which God am I serving as I negotiate, appropriate, critique, and develop the inherited customs and practices of my covenantal family? One who expects of me, created in God's image, to respond to the world in which I live? Or One who demands that I blind myself, replacing my singular point-of-view with the pre-approved vision of those who came before? How do I embrace a tradition that embraces a God who embraces life?

The tradition itself, compared by the midrash to "living waters," contains powerful and plentiful theological resources for responding to the shifting cultural landscapes of our ever-emerging historical drama. For too long these waters have sat stagnant, awaiting a community of inheritors, a living *tzibur*, sufficiently confident, willing, and thirsty to tap into them.

NOTES

1 Halakhic Spirituality

1. Abraham Joshua Heschel, *God in Search of Man: A Philosophy of Judaism* (New York: Farrar, Straus and Giroux, 1976), 348.
2. See David Hartman, *Israelis and the Jewish Tradition: An Ancient People Debating Its Future* (New Haven: Yale University Press, 2000), chapters 3–4.
3. See also Adiel Schremer, *The Lord Has Forsaken the Land: Radical Explanations of the Military and Political Defeat of the Jews in Tannaitic Literature* (New York: Oxford University Press, 2010).
4. Moses Maimonides, *Mishneh Torah*, Laws of Personality Development 3:2–3.
5. Moses Maimonides, *Guide for the Perplexed*, vol. 2, trans. Shlomo Pines (Chicago: University of Chicago Press, 1963), 619.
6. Abraham ben David, *Critical Glosses of the Ravad* on *Mishneh Torah*, The Laws of Repentance 3:7.
7. See Isadore Twersky, *Rabad of Posquieres: A Twelfth-Century Scholar* (Cambridge, MA: Harvard University Press, 1962).
8. Joseph B. Soloveitchik, "The Community," in *Tradition*, vol. 2, no.2, 7–25.

2 Toward a God-Intoxicated Halakha

1. Moses Maimonides, *Mishneh Torah*, Laws of Repentance 10:2–3.
2. Martin Buber, *Two Types of Faith* (New York: Harper Torchbooks, 1961), 131.
3. Moses Maimonides, *Guide for the Perplexed*, vol. 1, trans. Shlomo Pines (Chicago: University of Chicago Press, 1963), 123.
4. Maimonides, *Guide for the Perplexed*, vol. 2, 637.
5. Ibid., 327.
6. Pinchas Halevi, *Sefer Ha-Hinukh*, vol. 5:2, trans. Charles Wengrove (Jerusalem: Feldheim Publishers, 1992), 251.

3 Feminism and Apologetics

1. See Tova Hartman, *Feminism Encounters Traditional Judaism: Resistance and Accommodation* (Hanover, NH: Brandeis University Press, 2008), Introduction.

2. Joseph B. Soloveitchik, *Family Redeemed: Essays on Family Relationships* (Jersey City, NJ: KTAV, 2002), 17.

3. Ibid.

4. Ibid.

5. Ibid., 21.

6. Ibid.

7. Ibid.

8. Ibid., 21–22.

9. Ibid., 33.

10. Ibid., 22.

11. Ibid., 42

12. Pinchas Halevi, *Sefer Ha-Hinukh*, vol. 5 (Jerusalem: Feldheim Publishers, 1992).

13. Moses Maimonides, *Mishneh Torah*, Laws of Divorce 1.

14. Halevi, *Sefer Ha-Hinukh*, vol. 5, 225.

15. Ibid., 305.

16. The Talmud's gloss: "From here we learn the general rule that the honor/dignity of a woman is to dwell in the home" (BT *Yevamot* 77a).

17. Maimonides, *Mishneh Torah*, Laws of Marriage 15:17, 15:19.

18. Eliezer Berkowitz, *Jewish Women in Time and Torah* (Jersey City, NJ: KTAV, 1990), 1–2.

19. Ibid., 34.

20. Ibid., 56.

21. Maimonides, *Mishneh Torah*, Laws of Marriage 15:19–20.

22. Berkowitz, *Jewish Women in Time and Torah*, 56.

23. *Abudarham*, sec. 3, Blessings Before the Mitzvot.

24. Samson Raphael Hirsch, *Hirsch Commentary on the Torah* (Brooklyn: Judaica Press, 1989), Lev. 23:43.

25. Aaron Soloveitchik, *Logic of the Heart, Logic of the Mind: Wisdom and Reflections on Topics of Our Times* (Jerusalem: Genesis Jerusalem Press, 1991), 92.

26. Ibid., 93.

27. Ibid.

28. Ibid.

29. Ibid., 94.

30. Ibid., 96.

31. Ibid.

32. Ibid.

33. Ibid.

34. Ibid.

35. Ibid., 97.

36. Ibid., 93.
37. Samson Raphael Hirsch, *The Hirsch Siddur: The Order of Prayers for the Whole Year*, 2nd ed. (Nanuet, NY: Feldheim, 1978), 13.
38. Referred to here are the group of three morning blessings "… who has not made me a gentile … a slave … a woman."
39. Aaron Soloveitchik, *Logic of the Heart, Logic of the Mind*, 96–97.
40. Maimonides, *Mishneh Torah*, Laws of Torah Study 1:13.
41. Hartman, *Feminism Encounters Traditional Judaism*, 101–106.
42. Ibid., 104.
43. Ibid., 81–93.
44. Maimonides, *Mishneh Torah*, Laws of Kings 10:10.
45. Maimonides, *Mishneh Torah*, Laws of Slaves 9:8.

4 Biology or Covenant?

1. Moses Maimonides, *Mishneh Torah*, Laws of Forbidden Relations 14:1.
2. Ibid., 14:11.
3. Isadore Twersky, ed. A *Maimonides Reader* (Springfield, NJ: Behrman House, 1972), 475.
4. *Talmudic Encyclopedia*, s.v. "Ger," 173.
5. Or, possibly, a sociological one. We find a hint of the latter in the ruling that a fetus conceived by a non-Jewish woman who converts before the baby is born, is ruled to be Jewish. The reason given: while the biological dimension was unable to transmit Jewish sanctity ("unholy conception"), this lack is compensated for by the social dimension of being born into the lap of a Jewish community ("holy birth").
6. Twersky, *A Maimonides Reader*, 475–476.
7. Ibid.
8. While this ceremony is only ordained to take place during times when the Temple stands and the sacrificial rites are in effect, and is thus not practically applicable, Maimonides treats all such issues in the *Mishneh Torah*, which rules on any halakhic matter discussed in the Talmud.
9. Maimonides, *Mishneh Torah*, Laws of First-Fruit Offerings 1:3.
10. Maimonides, *Mishneh Torah*, Laws of Kings 1:4.

5 Where Did Modern Orthodoxy Go Wrong?

1. Emanuel Rackman, *Modern Halakha for Our Time* (Jersey City, NJ: KTAV, 1995), 71.
2. Ibid.
3. Ibid., 71–72.

4. Emanuel Rackman, "Halakha: Orthodox Approaches," in *Encyclopedia Judaica Year Book* 1975–76, ed. Cecil Roth (Jerusalem: Keter Publishing House, 1976), 143.

5. Ibid.

6. Ibid.

7. The scholar Lawrence Kaplan notes that Rackman himself argued that his approach could be supported within Soloveitchik's thought, based upon a close reading of some of his writings. See Lawrence Kaplan, "From Cooperation to Conflict: Rabbi Professor Emanuel Rackman, Rabbi Joseph B. Soloveitchik, and the Evolution of American Modern Orthodoxy, " in *Modern Judaism* 30, no. 1 (February 2010): 32.

8. Excerpted from the transcript from the 1975 convention of the Rabbinical Council of America.

9. Ibid.

10. Ibid.

11. Ibid.

12. Ibid.

13. Ibid.

6 The God Who Hates Lies

1. Moses Maimonides, *Mishneh Torah*, Laws of Forbidden Relations 14:1.

Suggestions for Further Reading

Berger, Peter L. *The Heretical Imperative: Contemporary Possibilities of Religious Affirmation.* New York: Doubleday, 1980.

Berkovitz, Eliezer. *Essential Essays on Judaism.* Jerusalem: Shalem Press, 2002.

Eisen, Arnold M. *Rethinking Modern Judaism: Ritual, Commandment, Community.* Chicago: University of Chicago Press, 1999.

Ellenson, David. *After Emancipation: Jewish Religious Responses to Modernity.* Cincinnati: Hebrew Union College Press, 2004.

Halbertal, Moshe. *People of the Book: Canon, Meaning, and Authority.* Cambridge, MA: Harvard University Press, 1997.

Hartman, David. *A Heart of Many Rooms: Celebrating the Many Voices within Judaism.* Woodstock, VT: Jewish Lights, 2002.

———. *A Living Covenant: The Innovative Spirit in Traditional Judaism.* Woodstock, VT: Jewish Lights, 1997.

———. *Love and Terror in the God Encounter: The Theological Legacy of Rabbi Joseph B. Soloveitchik.* Woodstock, VT: Jewish Lights, 2004.

Hartman, Tova. *Feminism Encounters Traditional Judaism: Resistance and Accommodation.* Hanover, NH: Brandeis University Press, 2007.

Idel, Moshe. *Old Worlds, New Mirrors: On Jewish Mysticism and Twentieth-Century Thought.* Philadelphia: University of Pennsylvania Press, 2010.

Kaplan, Mordecai M. *The Meaning of God in Modern Jewish Religion.* Detroit: Wayne State University Press, 1994.

Muffs, Yochanan. *The Personhood of God: Biblical Theology, Human Faith, and the Divine Image.* Woodstock, VT: Jewish Lights, 2005.

Rorty, Richard. *Philosophy and Social Hope.* New York: Penguin Books, 1999.

Soloveitchik, Joseph B. *Out of the Whirlwind: Essays on Mourning, Suffering, and the Human Condition.* Hoboken, NJ: KTAV, 2003.

Index

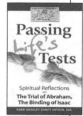
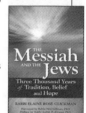

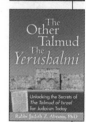

Congregation Resources

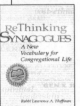

Jewish Megatrends: Charting the Course of the American Jewish Future
By Rabbi Sidney Schwarz; Foreword by Ambassador Stuart E. Eizenstat
Visionary solutions for a community ripe for transformational change—from fourteen leading innovators of Jewish life.
6 x 9, 288 pp, HC, 978-1-58023-667-6 **$24.99**

Relational Judaism: Using the Power of Relationships to Transform the Jewish Community *By Dr. Ron Wolfson*
How to transform the model of twentieth-century Jewish institutions into twenty-first-century relational communities offering meaning and purpose, belonging and blessing.
6 x 9, 288 pp, HC, 978-1-58023-666-9 **$24.99**

Revolution of Jewish Spirit: How to Revive *Ruakh* in Your Spiritual Life, Transform Your Synagogue & Inspire Your Jewish Community
By Rabbi Baruch HaLevi, DMin, and Ellen Frankel, LCSW; Foreword by Dr. Ron Wolfson
A practical and engaging guide to reinvigorating Jewish life. Offers strategies for sustaining and expanding transformation, impassioned leadership, inspired programming and inviting sacred spaces.
6 x 9, 224 pp, Quality PB Original, 978-1-58023-625-6 **$19.99**

Building a Successful Volunteer Culture: Finding Meaning in Service in the Jewish Community *By Rabbi Charles Simon; Foreword by Shelley Lindauer; Preface by Dr. Ron Wolfson*
6 x 9, 192 pp, Quality PB, 978-1-58023-408-5 **$16.99**

The Case for Jewish Peoplehood: Can We Be One?
By Dr. Erica Brown and Dr. Misha Galperin; Foreword by Rabbi Joseph Telushkin
6 x 9, 224 pp, HC, 978-1-58023-401-6 **$21.99**

Empowered Judaism: What Independent Minyanim Can Teach Us about Building Vibrant Jewish Communities *By Rabbi Elie Kaunfer; Foreword by Prof. Jonathan D. Sarna*
6 x 9, 224 pp, Quality PB, 978-1-58023-412-2 **$18.99**

Finding a Spiritual Home: How a New Generation of Jews Can Transform the American Synagogue *By Rabbi Sidney Schwarz*
6 x 9, 352 pp, Quality PB, 978-1-58023-185-5 **$19.95**

Inspired Jewish Leadership: Practical Approaches to Building Strong Communities
By Dr. Erica Brown 6 x 9, 256 pp, HC, 978-1-58023-361-3 **$27.99**

Jewish Pastoral Care, 2nd Edition: A Practical Handbook from Traditional & Contemporary Sources *Edited by Rabbi Dayle A. Friedman, MSW, MAJCS, BCC*
6 x 9, 528 pp, Quality PB, 978-1-58023-427-6 **$35.00**

Jewish Spiritual Direction: An Innovative Guide from Traditional and Contemporary Sources
Edited by Rabbi Howard A. Addison, PhD, and Barbara Eve Breitman, MSW
6 x 9, 368 pp, HC, 978-1-58023-230-2 **$30.00**

A Practical Guide to Rabbinic Counseling
Edited by Rabbi Yisrael N. Levitz, PhD, and Rabbi Abraham J. Twerski, MD
6 x 9, 432 pp, HC, 978-1-58023-562-4 **$40.00**

Professional Spiritual & Pastoral Care: A Practical Clergy and Chaplain's Handbook
Edited by Rabbi Stephen B. Roberts, MBA, MHL, BCJC
6 x 9, 480 pp, HC, 978-1-59473-312-3 **$50.00**

Reimagining Leadership in Jewish Organizations: Ten Practical Lessons to Help You Implement Change and Achieve Your Goals *By Dr. Misha Galperin*
6 x 9, 192 pp, Quality PB, 978-1-58023-492-4 **$16.99**

Rethinking Synagogues: A New Vocabulary for Congregational Life
By Rabbi Lawrence A. Hoffman, PhD 6 x 9, 240 pp, Quality PB, 978-1-58023-248-7 **$19.99**

Spiritual Community: The Power to Restore Hope, Commitment and Joy
By Rabbi David A. Teutsch, PhD
5½ x 8½, 144 pp, HC, 978-1-58023-270-8 **$19.99**

Spiritual Boredom: Rediscovering the Wonder of Judaism *By Dr. Erica Brown*
6 x 9, 208 pp, HC, 978-1-58023-405-4 **$21.99**

The Spirituality of Welcoming: How to Transform Your Congregation into a Sacred Community *By Dr. Ron Wolfson* 6 x 9, 224 pp, Quality PB, 978-1-58023-244-9 **$19.99**

Holidays / Holy Days

Prayers of Awe Series

An exciting new series that examines the High Holy Day liturgy to enrich the praying experience of everyone—whether experienced worshipers or guests who encounter Jewish prayer for the very first time.

May God Remember: Memory and Memorializing in Judaism—*Yizkor*
Edited by Rabbi Lawrence A. Hoffman, PhD
Examines the history and ideas behind *Yizkor*, the Jewish memorial service, and this fascinating chapter in Jewish piety.
6 x 9, 304 pp, HC, 978-1-58023-689-8 **$24.99**

We Have Sinned—Sin and Confession in Judaism: *Ashamnu and Al Chet*
Edited by Rabbi Lawrence A. Hoffman, PhD 6 x 9, 304 pp, HC, 978-1-58023-612-6 **$24.99**

Who by Fire, Who by Water—*Un'taneh Tokef*
Edited by Rabbi Lawrence A. Hoffman, PhD
6 x 9, 272 pp, Quality PB, 978-1-58023-672-0 **$19.99**; HC, 978-1-58023-424-5 **$24.99**

All These Vows—*Kol Nidre*
Edited by Rabbi Lawrence A. Hoffman, PhD 6 x 9, 288 pp, HC, 978-1-58023-430-6 **$24.99**

Rosh Hashanah Readings: Inspiration, Information and Contemplation
Yom Kippur Readings: Inspiration, Information and Contemplation
Edited by Rabbi Dov Peretz Elkins; Section Introductions from Arthur Green's These Are the Words
Rosh Hashanah: 6 x 9, 400 pp, Quality PB, 978-1-58023-437-5 **$19.99**
Yom Kippur: 6 x 9, 368 pp, Quality PB, 978-1-58023-438-2 **$19.99**; HC, 978-1-58023-271-5 **$24.99**

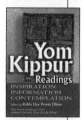

Reclaiming Judaism as a Spiritual Practice: Holy Days and Shabbat
By Rabbi Goldie Milgram 7 x 9, 272 pp, Quality PB, 978-1-58023-205-0 **$19.99**

The Sabbath Soul: Mystical Reflections on the Transformative Power of Holy Time
Selection, Translation and Commentary by Eitan Fishbane, PhD
6 x 9, 208 pp, Quality PB, 978-1-58023-459-7 **$18.99**

Shabbat, 2nd Edition: The Family Guide to Preparing for and Celebrating the Sabbath
By Dr. Ron Wolfson 7 x 9, 320 pp, Illus., Quality PB, 978-1-58023-164-0 **$21.99**

Hanukkah, 2nd Edition: The Family Guide to Spiritual Celebration
By Dr. Ron Wolfson 7 x 9, 240 pp, Illus., Quality PB, 978-1-58023-122-0 **$18.95**

Passover

My People's Passover Haggadah
Traditional Texts, Modern Commentaries
Edited by Rabbi Lawrence A. Hoffman, PhD, and David Arnow, PhD
A diverse and exciting collection of commentaries on the traditional Passover Haggadah—in two volumes!
Vol. 1: 7 x 10, 304 pp, HC, 978-1-58023-354-5 **$24.99**
Vol. 2: 7 x 10, 320 pp, HC, 978-1-58023-346-0 **$24.99**

Creating Lively Passover Seders, 2nd Edition: A Sourcebook of Engaging Tales, Texts & Activities *By David Arnow, PhD* 7 x 9, 464 pp, Quality PB, 978-1-58023-444-3 **$24.99**

Freedom Journeys: The Tale of Exodus and Wilderness across Millennia
By Rabbi Arthur O. Waskow and Rabbi Phyllis O. Berman
6 x 9, 288 pp, HC, 978-1-58023-445-0 **$24.99**

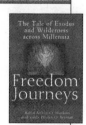

Leading the Passover Journey: The Seder's Meaning Revealed, the Haggadah's
Story Retold *By Rabbi Nathan Laufer*
6 x 9, 224 pp, Quality PB, 978-1-58023-399-6 **$18.99**

Passover, 2nd Edition: The Family Guide to Spiritual Celebration
By Dr. Ron Wolfson with Joel Lurie Grishaver 7 x 9, 416 pp, Quality PB, 978-1-58023-174-9 **$19.95**

The Women's Passover Companion: Women's Reflections on the Festival of Freedom
Edited by Rabbi Sharon Cohen Anisfeld, Tara Mohr and Catherine Spector; Foreword by Paula E. Hyman
6 x 9, 352 pp, Quality PB, 978-1-58023-231-9 **$19.99**; HC, 978-1-58023-128-2 **$24.95**

The Women's Seder Sourcebook: Rituals & Readings for Use at the Passover Seder
Edited by Rabbi Sharon Cohen Anisfeld, Tara Mohr and Catherine Spector
6 x 9, 384 pp, Quality PB, 978-1-58023-232-6 **$19.99**

Social Justice

Where Justice Dwells
A Hands-On Guide to Doing Social Justice in Your Jewish Community
By Rabbi Jill Jacobs; Foreword by Rabbi David Saperstein
Provides ways to envision and act on your own ideals of social justice.
7 x 9, 288 pp, Quality PB Original, 978-1-58023-453-5 **$24.99**

There Shall Be No Needy
Pursuing Social Justice through Jewish Law and Tradition
By Rabbi Jill Jacobs; Foreword by Rabbi Elliot N. Dorff, PhD; Preface by Simon Greer
Confronts the most pressing issues of twenty-first-century America from a deeply Jewish perspective. 6 x 9, 288 pp, Quality PB, 978-1-58023-425-2 **$16.99**

There Shall Be No Needy Teacher's Guide 8½ x 11, 56 pp, PB, 978-1-58023-429-0 **$8.99**

Conscience
The Duty to Obey and the Duty to Disobey
By Rabbi Harold M. Schulweis
Examines the idea of conscience and the role conscience plays in our relationships to government, law, ethics, religion, human nature, God—and to each other.
6 x 9, 160 pp, Quality PB, 978-1-58023-419-1 **$16.99**; HC, 978-1-58023-375-0 **$19.99**

Judaism and Justice
The Jewish Passion to Repair the World
By Rabbi Sidney Schwarz; Foreword by Ruth Messinger
Explores the relationship between Judaism, social justice and the Jewish identity of American Jews. 6 x 9, 352 pp, Quality PB, 978-1-58023-353-8 **$19.99**

Spirituality / Women's Interest

New Jewish Feminism
Probing the Past, Forging the Future
Edited by Rabbi Elyse Goldstein; Foreword by Anita Diamant
Looks at the growth and accomplishments of Jewish feminism and what they mean for Jewish women today and tomorrow.
6 x 9, 480 pp, HC, 978-1-58023-359-0 **$24.99**

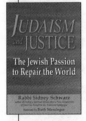

The Divine Feminine in Biblical Wisdom Literature
Selections Annotated & Explained
Translation & Annotation by Rabbi Rami Shapiro
5½ x 8½, 240 pp, Quality PB, 978-1-59473-109-9 **$16.99**
(A book from SkyLight Paths, Jewish Lights' sister imprint)

The Quotable Jewish Woman
Wisdom, Inspiration & Humor from the Mind & Heart
Edited by Elaine Bernstein Partnow
6 x 9, 496 pp, Quality PB, 978-1-58023-236-4 **$19.99**

The Women's Haftarah Commentary
New Insights from Women Rabbis on the 54 Weekly Haftarah Portions, the 5 Megillot & Special Shabbatot
Edited by Rabbi Elyse Goldstein
Illuminates the historical significance of female portrayals in the Haftarah and the Five Megillot. 6 x 9, 560 pp, Quality PB, 978-1-58023-371-2 **$19.99**

The Women's Torah Commentary
New Insights from Women Rabbis on the 54 Weekly Torah Portions
Edited by Rabbi Elyse Goldstein
Over fifty women rabbis offer inspiring insights on the Torah, in a week-by-week format.
6 x 9, 496 pp, Quality PB, 978-1-58023-370-5 **$19.99**; HC, 978-1-58023-076-6 **$34.95**

See Passover for *The Women's Passover Companion: Women's Reflections on the Festival of Freedom* and *The Women's Seder Sourcebook: Rituals & Readings for Use at the Passover Seder*.

Theology / Philosophy

Believing and Its Tensions: A Personal Conversation about God, Torah, Suffering and Death in Jewish Thought
By Rabbi Neil Gillman, PhD
Explores the changing nature of belief and the complexities of reconciling the intellectual, emotional and moral questions of Gillman's own searching mind and soul.
5½ x 8½, 144 pp, HC, 978-1-58023-669-0 **$19.99**

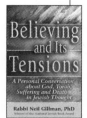

God of Becoming and Relationship: The Dynamic Nature of Process Theology *By Rabbi Bradley Shavit Artson, DHL*
Explains how Process Theology breaks us free from the strictures of ancient Greek and medieval European philosophy, allowing us to see all creation as related patterns of energy through which we connect to everything.
6 x 9, 208 pp, HC, 978-1-58023-713-0 **$24.99**

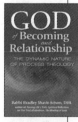

The Other Talmud—The Yerushalmi: Unlocking the Secrets of The Talmud of Israel for Judaism Today *By Rabbi Judith Z. Abrams, PhD*
A fascinating—and stimulating—look at "the other Talmud" and the possibilities for Jewish life reflected there. 6 x 9, 256 pp, HC, 978-1-58023-463-4 **$24.99**

The Way of Man: According to Hasidic Teaching
By Martin Buber; New Translation and Introduction by Rabbi Bernard H. Mehlman and Dr. Gabriel E. Padawer; Foreword by Paul Mendes-Flohr
An accessible and engaging new translation of Buber's classic work—*available as an e-book only.* E-book, 978-1-58023-601-0 Digital List Price **$14.99**

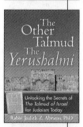

The Death of Death: Resurrection and Immortality in Jewish Thought
By Rabbi Neil Gillman, PhD 6 x 9, 336 pp, Quality PB, 978-1-58023-081-0 **$18.95**

Doing Jewish Theology: God, Torah & Israel in Modern Judaism *By Rabbi Neil Gillman, PhD*
6 x 9, 304 pp, Quality PB, 978-1-58023-439-9 **$18.99**; HC, 978-1-58023-322-4 **$24.99**

From Defender to Critic: The Search for a New Jewish Self
By Dr. David Hartman 6 x 9, 336 pp, HC, 978-1-58023-515-0 **$35.00**

The God Who Hates Lies: Confronting & Rethinking Jewish Tradition
By Dr. David Hartman with Charlie Buckholtz 6 x 9, 208 pp, HC, 978-1-58023-455-9 **$24.99**

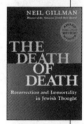

A Heart of Many Rooms: Celebrating the Many Voices within Judaism
By Dr. David Hartman 6 x 9, 352 pp, Quality PB, 978-1-58023-156-5 **$19.95**

Jewish Theology in Our Time: A New Generation Explores the Foundations and Future of Jewish Belief *Edited by Rabbi Elliot J. Cosgrove, PhD; Foreword by Rabbi David J. Wolpe; Preface by Rabbi Carole B. Balin, PhD* 6 x 9, 240 pp, Quality PB, 978-1-58023-630-1, **$19.99**; HC, 978-1-58023-413-9 **$24.99**

Maimonides—Essential Teachings on Jewish Faith & Ethics: The Book of Knowledge & the Thirteen Principles of Faith—Annotated & Explained
Translation and Annotation by Rabbi Marc D. Angel, PhD
5½ x 8½, 224 pp, Quality PB Original, 978-1-59473-311-6 **$18.99***

Maimonides, Spinoza and Us: Toward an Intellectually Vibrant Judaism
By Rabbi Marc D. Angel, PhD 6 x 9, 224 pp, HC, 978-1-58023-411-5 **$24.99**

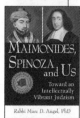

Our Religious Brains: What Cognitive Science Reveals about Belief, Morality, Community and Our Relationship with God
By Rabbi Ralph D. Mecklenburger; Foreword by Dr. Howard Kelfer; Preface by Dr. Neil Gillman
6 x 9, 224 pp, HC, 978-1-58023-508-2 **$24.99**

Your Word Is Fire: The Hasidic Masters on Contemplative Prayer
Edited and translated by Rabbi Arthur Green, PhD, and Barry W. Holtz
6 x 9, 160 pp, Quality PB, 978-1-879045-25-5 **$16.99**

I Am Jewish
Personal Reflections Inspired by the Last Words of Daniel Pearl
Almost 150 Jews—both famous and not—from all walks of life, from all around the world, write about many aspects of their Judaism.
Edited by Judea and Ruth Pearl 6 x 9, 304 pp, Deluxe PB w/ flaps, 978-1-58023-259-3 **$19.99**
Download a free copy of the *I Am Jewish Teacher's Guide* at www.jewishlights.com.

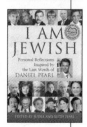

*A book from SkyLight Paths, Jewish Lights' sister imprint

Spirituality / Prayer

Davening: A Guide to Meaningful Jewish Prayer
By Rabbi Zalman Schachter-Shalomi with Joel Segel; Foreword by Rabbi Lawrence Kushner
A fresh approach to prayer for all who wish to appreciate the power of prayer's poetry, song and ritual, and to join the age-old conversation that Jews have had with God. 6 x 9, 240 pp, Quality PB, 978-1-58023-627-0 **$18.99**

Jewish Men Pray: Words of Yearning, Praise, Petition, Gratitude and Wonder from Traditional and Contemporary Sources
Edited by Rabbi Kerry M. Olitzky and Stuart M. Matlins; Foreword by Rabbi Bradley Shavit Artson, DHL
A celebration of Jewish men's voices in prayer—to strengthen, heal, comfort, and inspire—from the ancient world up to our own day.
5 x 7¼, 400 pp, HC, 978-1-58023-628-7 **$19.99**

Making Prayer Real: Leading Jewish Spiritual Voices on Why Prayer Is Difficult and What to Do about It *By Rabbi Mike Comins* 6 x 9, 320 pp, Quality PB, 978-1-58023-417-7 **$18.99**

Witnesses to the One: The Spiritual History of the *Sh'ma*
By Rabbi Joseph B. Meszler; Foreword by Rabbi Elyse Goldstein
6 x 9, 176 pp, Quality PB, 978-1-58023-400-9 **$16.99**; HC, 978-1-58023-309-5 **$19.99**

My People's Prayer Book Series: Traditional Prayers, Modern
Commentaries *Edited by Rabbi Lawrence A. Hoffman, PhD*
Provides diverse and exciting commentary to the traditional liturgy. Will help you find new wisdom in Jewish prayer, and bring liturgy into your life. Each book includes Hebrew text, modern translations and commentaries from all perspectives of the Jewish world.

Vol. 1—The *Sh'ma* and Its Blessings
  7 x 10, 168 pp, HC, 978-1-879045-79-8 **$29.99**
Vol. 2—The *Amidah* 7 x 10, 240 pp, HC, 978-1-879045-80-4 **$24.95**
Vol. 3—*P'sukei D'zimrah* (Morning Psalms)
  7 x 10, 240 pp, HC, 978-1-879045-81-1 **$29.99**
Vol. 4—*Seder K'riat Hatorah* (The Torah Service)
  7 x 10, 264 pp, HC, 978-1-879045-82-8 **$29.99**
Vol. 5—*Birkhot Hashachar* (Morning Blessings)
  7 x 10, 240 pp, HC, 978-1-879045-83-5 **$24.95**
Vol. 6—*Tachanun* and Concluding Prayers
  7 x 10, 240 pp, HC, 978-1-879045-84-2 **$24.95**
Vol. 7—Shabbat at Home 7 x 10, 240 pp, HC, 978-1-879045-85-9 **$24.95**
Vol. 8—*Kabbalat Shabbat* (Welcoming Shabbat in the Synagogue)
  7 x 10, 240 pp, HC, 978-1-58023-121-3 **$24.99**
Vol. 9—Welcoming the Night: *Minchah* and *Ma'ariv* (Afternoon and
  Evening Prayer) 7 x 10, 272 pp, HC, 978-1-58023-262-3 **$24.99**
Vol. 10—Shabbat Morning: *Shacharit* and *Musaf* (Morning and
  Additional Services) 7 x 10, 240 pp, HC, 978-1-58023-240-1 **$29.99**

Spirituality / Lawrence Kushner

I'm God; You're Not: Observations on Organized Religion & Other Disguises of the Ego
6 x 9, 256 pp, Quality PB, 978-1-58023-513-6 **$18.99**; HC, 978-1-58023-441-2 **$21.99**

The Book of Letters: A Mystical Hebrew Alphabet
Popular HC Edition, 6 x 9, 80 pp, 2-color text, 978-1-879045-00-2 **$24.95**
Collector's Limited Edition, 9 x 12, 80 pp, gold-foil-embossed pages, w/ limited-edition silkscreened print, 978-1-879045-04-0 **$349.00**

The Book of Miracles: A Young Person's Guide to Jewish Spiritual Awareness
6 x 9, 96 pp, 2-color illus., HC, 978-1-879045-78-1 **$16.95** *For ages 9–13*

God Was in This Place & I, i Did Not Know: Finding Self, Spirituality and
Ultimate Meaning 6 x 9, 192 pp, Quality PB, 978-1-879045-33-0 **$16.95**

Honey from the Rock: An Introduction to Jewish Mysticism
6 x 9, 176 pp, Quality PB, 978-1-58023-073-5 **$16.95**

Invisible Lines of Connection: Sacred Stories of the Ordinary
5½ x 8½, 160 pp, Quality PB, 978-1-879045-98-9 **$16.99**

The Way Into Jewish Mystical Tradition
6 x 9, 224 pp, Quality PB, 978-1-58023-200-5 **$18.99**; HC, 978-1-58023-029-2 **$21.95**

Spirituality

Amazing Chesed: Living a Grace-Filled Judaism
By Rabbi Rami Shapiro Drawing from ancient and contemporary, traditional and non-traditional Jewish wisdom, reclaims the idea of grace in Judaism.
6 x 9, 176 pp, Quality PB, 978-1-58023-624-9 **$16.99**

Jewish with Feeling: A Guide to Meaningful Jewish Practice
By Rabbi Zalman Schachter-Shalomi with Joel Segel
Takes off from basic questions like "Why be Jewish?" and whether the word God still speaks to us today and lays out a vision for a whole-person Judaism.
5½ x 8½, 288 pp, Quality PB, 978-1-58023-691-1 **$19.99**

Perennial Wisdom for the Spiritually Independent: Sacred Teachings—Annotated & Explained   *Annotation by Rami Shapiro; Foreword by Richard Rohr*
Weaves sacred texts and teachings from the world's major religions into a coherent exploration of the five core questions at the heart of every religion's search.
5½ x 8½, 336 pp, Quality PB Original, 978-1-59473-515-8 **$16.99**

Aleph-Bet Yoga: Embodying the Hebrew Letters for Physical and Spiritual Well-Being
By Steven A. Rapp; Foreword by Tamar Frankiel, PhD, and Judy Greenfeld; Preface by Hart Lazer
7 x 10, 128 pp, b/w photos, Quality PB, Lay-flat binding, 978-1-58023-162-6 **$16.95**

A Book of Life: Embracing Judaism as a Spiritual Practice
By Rabbi Michael Strassfeld 6 x 9, 544 pp, Quality PB, 978-1-58023-247-0 **$19.99**

Bringing the Psalms to Life: How to Understand and Use the Book of Psalms
By Rabbi Daniel F. Polish, PhD 6 x 9, 208 pp, Quality PB, 978-1-58023-157-2 **$16.95**

Does the Soul Survive? A Jewish Journey to Belief in Afterlife, Past Lives & Living with Purpose   *By Rabbi Elie Kaplan Spitz; Foreword by Brian L. Weiss, MD*
6 x 9, 288 pp, Quality PB, 978-1-58023-165-7 **$18.99**

Entering the Temple of Dreams: Jewish Prayers, Movements and Meditations for the End of the Day   *By Tamar Frankiel, PhD, and Judy Greenfeld*
7 x 10, 192 pp, illus., Quality PB, 978-1-58023-079-7 **$16.95**

First Steps to a New Jewish Spirit: Reb Zalman's Guide to Recapturing the Intimacy & Ecstasy in Your Relationship with God *By Rabbi Zalman M. Schachter-Shalomi with Donald Gropman* 6 x 9, 144 pp, Quality PB, 978-1-58023-182-4 **$16.95**

Foundations of Sephardic Spirituality: The Inner Life of Jews of the Ottoman Empire
By Rabbi Marc D. Angel, PhD 6 x 9, 224 pp, Quality PB, 978-1-58023-341-5 **$18.99**

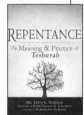

God & the Big Bang: Discovering Harmony between Science & Spirituality
By Dr. Daniel C. Matt 6 x 9, 216 pp, Quality PB, 978-1-879045-89-7 **$18.99**

God in Our Relationships: Spirituality between People from the Teachings of Martin Buber *By Rabbi Dennis S. Ross* 5½ x 8½, 160 pp, Quality PB, 978-1-58023-147-3 **$16.95**

The Jewish Lights Spirituality Handbook: A Guide to Understanding, Exploring & Living a Spiritual Life *Edited by Stuart M. Matlins*
6 x 9, 456 pp, Quality PB, 978-1-58023-093-3 **$19.99**

Judaism, Physics and God: Searching for Sacred Metaphors in a Post-Einstein World
By Rabbi David W. Nelson 6 x 9, 352 pp, Quality PB, inc. reader's discussion guide,
978-1-58023-306-4 **$18.99**; HC, 352 pp, 978-1-58023-252-4 **$24.99**

Meaning & Mitzvah: Daily Practices for Reclaiming Judaism through Prayer, God, Torah, Hebrew, Mitzvot and Peoplehood *By Rabbi Goldie Milgram*
7 x 9, 336 pp, Quality PB, 978-1-58023-256-2 **$19.99**

Repentance: The Meaning and Practice of Teshuvah
By Dr. Louis E. Newman; Foreword by Rabbi Harold M. Schulweis; Preface by Rabbi Karyn D. Kedar
6 x 9, 256 pp, HC, 978-1-58023-426-9 **$24.99** Quality PB, 978-1-58023-718-5 **$18.99**

The Sabbath Soul: Mystical Reflections on the Transformative Power of Holy Time
Selection, Translation and Commentary by Eitan Fishbane, PhD
6 x 9, 208 pp, Quality PB, 978-1-58023-459-7 **$18.99**

Tanya, the Masterpiece of Hasidic Wisdom: Selections Annotated & Explained
Translation & Annotation by Rabbi Rami Shapiro; Foreword by Rabbi Zalman M. Schachter-Shalomi
5½ x 8½, 240 pp, Quality PB, 978-1-59473-275-1 **$16.99**

These Are the Words, 2nd Edition: A Vocabulary of Jewish Spiritual Life
By Rabbi Arthur Green, PhD 6 x 9, 320 pp, Quality PB, 978-1-58023-494-8 **$19.99**

About Jewish Lights

People of all faiths and backgrounds yearn for books that attract, engage, educate, and spiritually inspire.

Our principal goal is to stimulate thought and help all people learn about who the Jewish People are, where they come from, and what the future can be made to hold. While people of our diverse Jewish heritage are the primary audience, our books speak to people in the Christian world as well and will broaden their understanding of Judaism and the roots of their own faith.

We bring to you authors who are at the forefront of spiritual thought and experience. While each has something different to say, they all say it in a voice that you can hear.

Our books are designed to welcome you and then to engage, stimulate, and inspire. We judge our success not only by whether or not our books are beautiful and commercially successful, but by whether or not they make a difference in your life.

For your information and convenience, at the back of this book we have provided a list of other Jewish Lights books you might find interesting and useful. They cover all the categories of your life:

Bar/Bat Mitzvah
Bible Study / Midrash
Children's Books
Congregation Resources
Current Events / History
Ecology / Environment
Fiction: Mystery, Science Fiction
Grief / Healing
Holidays / Holy Days
Inspiration
Kabbalah / Mysticism / Enneagram

Life Cycle
Meditation
Men's Interest
Parenting
Prayer / Ritual / Sacred Practice
Social Justice
Spirituality
Theology / Philosophy
Travel
Twelve Steps
Women's Interest

Stuart M. Matlins, Publisher